THE COST OF DOING BU$INESS STUDY, 2022 EDITION

NAHB®
National Association of Home Builders

The Cost of Doing Business Study, 2022 Edition

BuilderBooks, a Service of the National Association of Home Builders

Patricia Potts	Senior Director
Joe Rudden	Cover Design
Robert Brown	Composition
Gerald M. Howard	Chief Executive Officer
Robert Dietz	Senior Vice President and Chief Economist, Economics and Housing Policy
Paul Emrath	Vice President, Economics and Housing Policy
Rose Quint	Assistant Vice President, Survey Research, Economics and Housing Policy
Marcia Childs	Director, Business Management Department

Published in the United States of America

25 24 23 22 1 2 3 4 5

ISBN-13: 978-0-86718-789-2
eISBN-13: 978-0-86718-790-8

For further information, please contact:
National Association of Home Builders
1201 15th Street, NW
Washington, DC 20005-2800
BuilderBooks.com

Contents

Figures

Chapter 1. All Survey Respondents

Chapter 2. Builders with Land Costs

Chapter 3. Builders without Land Costs

Chapter 4. Combination Builders

Chapter 5. Small-Volume Builders

Chapter 6. Production Builders

Chapter 7. Builder Financial Performance by Region and Business Model

Chapter 8. Operations

Chapter 9. Historical Data and Trends

Tables

Chapter 1. All Survey Respondents

Chapter 2. Builders with Land Costs

Chapter 3. Builders without Land Costs

Chapter 4. Combination Builders

Chapter 5. Small-Volume Builders

Chapter 6. Production Builders

Chapter 9. Historical Data and Trends

Acknowledgments

The NAHB Economics and Housing Policy Group conducted the survey and tabulated the findings. The NAHB Business Management and Information Technology Committee provided oversight since it has jurisdiction over matters relating to improving the business management skills of NAHB's builder members in order to enhance their competitiveness, profitability, and professionalism.

In accordance with the NAHB strategic plan objectives, the committee makes policy recommendations on business management issues, develops educational programs, writes and publishes manuals, conducts business management research, and provides consulting assistance to other committees.

The Committee's mission statement is

> *"To serve as the leading resource to the building industry in the areas of management, finance, information technology, operations, and human resources."*

Members of the 2021 Business Management & Information Technology Committee

Thomas Baalmann, B & B Lumber Co

Vince Butler, CAPS, CGR, GMB, GMR, Butler Brothers Corp

Cynthia Cepko, CMP, CSP, Master CSP, MIRM, Granite Homes Property Management

Don Colegrove, CGP, University of Louisiana-Monroe

Darylene Dennon, Solid Energy, Inc.

Joyce Duerfeldt, Nationwide Contractors' Alliance

Teri Edwards, Onslow County HBA

John Gunkelman, CAPS, CGB, CGP, CGR, Dakota Construction of Fargo, Inc.

Alan Hanbury Jr., CAPS, CGR, GMR, House of Hanbury

Robert Hanbury, Construction Solutions Consultant, LLC
Connelly Hayward, CGB, CGP, Triumph Homes, LLC
John Jones, SoftPlan Systems, Inc.
Joel Katz, Katz Builders, Inc.
Gary Kerns, Gary Kerns Homebuilders, LLC
Chuck Miller, CAPS, CGB, CGP, CGR, CMP, CSP, GMB, GMR, Master CSP, MIRM, Chuck Miller Consulting, LLC
Russ Pies, Builders FirstSource
Michael Theunissen, Howling Hammer Builders, Inc.
Ron Wanless, Technology Design Associates
Kerry White, HomeQuest Properties, Inc.
Kevin Woodward, Legacy Homes, Inc.

We also thank the following contributing writers and reviewers:
Joyce Duerfeldt, Nationwide Contractors' Alliance Inc.
Alan Hanbury Jr., CAPS, CGP, CGR, GMR
Steven W. Hays, Sr., CPA, RubinBrown, LLC
Carrie Roeger, White Stone Residential, LLC

We thank those builders who provided their valuable financial information for this 20th edition in *The Cost of Doing Business Study* series. Without their time and effort, this study would not have been possible.

NAHB strives to make *The Cost of Doing Business Study* a useful tool for understanding the home building industry and helping builders improve their businesses. If you have comments or suggestions for the next edition of the study, please contact NAHB's Business Management Department at 800-368-5242 or e-mail businessmanagement@nahb.org.

Introduction

The financial performance of any company is directly linked to the industry environment in which it operates. Factors such as the number and size of its competitors, barriers to enter or exit, capital requirements, economies of scale, or the bargaining power of customers and suppliers all play a role in the potential profitability of a company. Given this reality, one of the most useful strategies to evaluate a company's competitiveness is to compare its financial performance against profitability benchmarks for the industry as a whole. In order to create such reference points, the National Association of Home Builders periodically conducts the *Cost of Doing Business Study* — a nationwide survey of single-family builders designed to produce exactly those profitability benchmarks for the home building industry.

The Cost of Doing Business Study provides information that will help you with resource allocation, budgeting, and target setting for various costs and expense lines, but more broadly, the study can help you create an overall strategy to achieve higher financial results in the future. By providing recent and reliable data on industrywide profit margins and financial ratios, the study helps builders remain (or become) successful in today's competitive environment.

How the Study was Prepared

The Cost of Doing Business Study survey questionnaire was sent electronically to more than 7,500 companies in April of 2021. The questionnaire asked for 2020 financial and operational information as well as details about the type of single-family units closed in 2020. The analysis presented in *The Cost of Doing Business Study* is based only on responses from builders who reported their main operation to be single-family production or custom home building (either on owners' lots or builders' lots). NAHB received 607 partial or complete responses, as not every question was answered by all respondents. Survey responses are categorically confidential, and at no point is any company-specific information revealed. Only aggregate calculations are published and survey respondents remain anonymous.

Organization of the Study

Nine chapters of study results and two related chapters comprise *The Cost of Doing Business Study,* 2022 Edition. The study is organized as follows:

Chapters 1–6 provide detailed information on gross profit, net profit, assets, liabilities, owner's equity, and financial ratios. Chapter 1 provides this information aggregated for all survey respondents, including a comparison between the top 25% and bottom 25% of builders. Subsequent chapters present the data for specific types of companies, such as small-volume and production builders.

Chapter 7 compares builders' performance by geographic region and business model (builders with land cost, without land cost, and combination builders). Chapter 8 provides data about the main operation of respondents, years in business, and number of units closed in 2020. Chapter 9 discusses historical trends based on data from *The Cost of Doing Business Study,* NAHB's Construction Costs surveys, and financial data available from select public builders.

How to Use the Study

The Cost of Doing Business Study contains a wealth of information about the residential construction industry, but it is much more than a statistical report. Builders can use the study as a benchmark for their businesses by comparing their net profit to the industry average, or better yet, to the top most profitable quartile! A company's ability to consistently generate adequate net profit strongly influences whether it will be successful in the long-run.

By aggregating information about earnings in the home building industry, the study allows builders to analyze their financial performance, determine whether they are optimally managing their business, and assess whether they are achieving their business goals. The study helps company owners pinpoint areas for improvement, set budget targets, and create a road map for boosting profitability and increasing efficiency. The study breaks down survey findings by region, 2020 dollar revenue, number of units closed, and whether builders have land costs. Where applicable, the study also shows results for the top and bottom quartiles (in terms of net profit performance). It also shows the average performance for all builders within a size category i.e. small (1 to 25 closings) vs. production (26+ closings) builders. In addition, the study compares data from the most recent survey (2020 fiscal year data) with the previous two surveys (2014 and 2017 data).

To get maximum value from this study, gather your financial information, including your income statement and balance sheet, and see how your performance compared with that of other builders. Once you have analyzed your company's performance compared with the aggregate for similar companies, you can use the findings to make better business decisions and influence the behavior of others who impact your company's success or failure. For example, you can use the study as a selling point to lenders. If your company performs better than or even at the same level as the industry average, present these facts to negotiate better loan terms or interest rates. Also use the findings to motivate your employees. For example, you can use industry averages as the basic performance level for rewarding employees with merit increases or bonuses.

Industry Profitability

On average, single-family builders reported declines in both gross and net profit margins between 2017 and 2020:

- The average gross profit declined from 19.0% in 2017 to 18.2% in 2020.
- The average net profit declined from 7.6% to 7.0% during the same period.

Gross profit equals sales minus the cost of sales. Cost of sales comprises

- materials and labor used in a home's construction;
- land on which the home is built; and
- indirect construction costs (field or construction expenses) that cannot be tied to a specific home.

Gross profit is measured before deducting operating expenses (financing, sales and marketing, general and administrative, depreciation, and owner's compensation). Here's how to calculate gross profit as a percentage of revenue:

1. Subtract the cost of sales from total sales (revenue).
2. Divide that gross profit by total sales (revenue).

The following example calculates gross profit margin for a company with $2,000,000 in total sales (revenue) and $1,400,000 in cost of sales.

$2,000,000 – $1,400,000 = $600,000

$600,000 ¸ $2,000,000 = 0.30 or 30%

You can (and should) calculate gross profit at all operational levels—by home, by community, and for all jobs over the course of a year.

Net profit is the income from sales after deducting the cost of sales, expenses, and owner's compensation. In other words, net profit is the money a business earns after it has paid all the costs of both the project (hard costs) and the operating expenses (soft costs). When comparing your net profits with the overall industry performance, it is best to consider the pretax net profits because many factors (not discussed in this study) determine the taxes a business pays.

Consider the same company in which total sales are $2,000,000; cost of sales, or cost of goods sold, is $1,400,000; and operating expenses plus owner's compensation total $400,000. As described earlier, the gross profit is $600,000, a gross margin of 30%. Operating expenses take up 20% of total sales, leaving a net profit of $200,000, a net profit margin of 10%. To calculate the net profit as a percentage of sales, subtract the cost of sales, operating expenses, and owner's compensation from total sales, and then divide that net profit by total sales as follows:

$2,000,000 – $1,400,000 – $400,000 = $200,000

$200,000 ¸ $2,000,000 = .1 or 10%.

Applying the Information to Your Business

What is an acceptable profit margin? There really is no ideal number, but industry experts suggest aiming for gross profit margins of 22–27% and net profits of 8–15%. Although many companies post higher numbers, others do not achieve these levels. The averages presented in *The Cost of Doing Business Study* aren't necessarily appropriate goals for every company. To determine your profit goals, consider your level of risk, the cyclical nature of the industry, and the return you could get for your capital if you invested it in another business sector or in a money market account.

Be cautious when considering changing your business plan based on information in this publication. Consider not only the benefits of the proposed change, but its costs. For example, although you could raise your home sales price to increase your profit margin that is not a sustainable strategy for growing your bottom line. Because your homes probably would be too expensive for the market, your sales velocity would slow or stop.

Although *The Cost of Doing Business Study* is an essential resource to help you manage your business more effectively and profitably, you need other tools as well. These include your annual operating budget, which you can use to evaluate monthly financial performance. You also need tools to monitor construction quality, employee or trade contractor performance, schedules, and pre- and post-construction systems. When you measure performance in essential areas, you will have the information needed to improve management, quality, and profitability.

1

All Survey Respondents

The financial performance of any company is directly linked to the industry environment in which it operates. Factors such as the number and size of its competitors, barriers to enter or exit, capital requirements, economies of scale, or the bargaining power of customers and suppliers all play a role in the potential profitability of a company. Given this reality, one of the most useful strategies to evaluate a company's competitiveness is to compare its financial performance against profitability benchmarks for the industry as a whole. In order to create such reference points, the National Association of Home Builders periodically conducts *The Cost of Doing Business Study* — a nationwide survey of single-family builders designed to produce exactly those profitability benchmarks for the home building industry.

In all, more than 7,500 builder members received the survey electronically in April 2021, requesting their company's income statement and balance sheet for fiscal year 2020. The sample was stratified to accurately represent builders across the four Census regions of the country and also across builder size categories (in terms of number of single-family units built). A total of 672 responses were received, but not all questions were answered by every respondent.

The financial analysis presented throughout *The Cost of Doing Business Study* is based solely on responses from builders who reported their main operation to be single-family home building, whether production or custom (on the owner's or builder's lots). Table 1.1 breaks down the responses by U.S. Census region, type of builder, number of single-family homes closed in 2020, and total 2020 revenue.[1]

Table 1.1. Respondents' profile

Region	**% of total**
Northeast: Connecticut, Maine, Massachusetts, New Hampshire, New Jersey, New York, Pennsylvania, Rhode Island, Vermont	7
Midwest: Illinois, Indiana, Iowa, Kansas, Michigan, Minnesota, Missouri, Nebraska, North Dakota, Ohio, South Dakota, Wisconsin	21
South: Alabama, Arkansas, Delaware, District of Columbia, Florida, Georgia, Kentucky, Louisiana, Maryland, Mississippi, North Carolina, Oklahoma, South Carolina, Tennessee, Texas, Virginia, West Virginia	53
West: Alaska, Arizona, California, Colorado, Hawaii, Idaho, Montana, Nevada, New Mexico, Oregon, Utah, Washington, Wyoming	18
Type of builder	
With land costs	35
Without land costs	19
Combination	46
Single-family homes closed in 2020	
<10	46
10–25	30
26–99	17
≥100	7
Total 2020 revenue	
< $2 million	26
$2 to $9.9 million	36
$10 million+	38

[1] Due to rounding, the numbers in the tables presented throughout the study may not add up to 100%.

Fifty-three percent of the study's respondents operate in the South, followed by 21% in the Midwest and 18% in the West. Only 7% of respondents are based in the Northeast. This breakdown reasonably reflects the actual distribution of single-family housing starts across regions of the U.S. in 2020 (South: 56%; West: 24%; Midwest: 14%; and Northeast: 6%).

When analyzed by type of builder, 35% of respondents were builders with land costs – defined in this study as those who only build speculative or pre-sold homes on lots they own. Another 19% were builders *without land costs* — defined as those who build exclusively on lots owned by their customers. The remaining 46% were *combination* builders — defined as those who build homes on their own lots as well as on their customers' lots.

For the purpose of this study, *small-volume* builders are those with 25 or fewer closings in 2020, and production builders are those with 26 or more closings. A total of 76% of all respondents were small-volume builders. Within that group, 46% closed fewer than 10 homes and 30% closed 10 to 25 homes. Of the 24% who were production builders, 17% closed 26 to 99 units and 7% closed 100 units or more.

The rest of this chapter provides detailed information on gross profit, net profit, assets, liabilities, owner's equity, and financial ratios aggregated for all builders in the study, including a comparison between the top 25% most successful and the bottom 25% least successful builders (in terms of net margins). Subsequent chapters present the data for specific types of companies, such as small-volume or production builders.

Balance Sheet and Income Statement

The Cost of Doing Business Study survey asked respondents for data from their 2020 income statement, including details about revenue, cost of sales and expenses. On the revenue side, the survey requested information about income generated from single-family and multifamily building, as well as from residential remodeling and light commercial/industrial building. In terms of cost of sales, builders were asked to provide land costs and both direct and indirect construction costs. Data on operating expenses were requested for financing expenses, sales and marketing expenses, general and administrative expenses, depreciation, and owner's compensation.

In addition to the income statement, the survey also inquired about builders' 2020 balance sheets. More specifically, it asked about how much money was held in cash, how much in receivables and inventories, the amount tied to construction work in progress, as well as the amounts owed in current liabilities, construction loans, and long-term liabilities, along with the total amount held as owner's equity.

To provide historical context for the current findings, this study compares the 2020 data with results from the previous two editions of *The Cost of Doing Business Study* (covering fiscal years 2014 and 2017). Before delving into results, it is important to highlight the fact that 2020 was not a normal year for any person or business in any part of the world, as the COVID-19 pandemic engulfed our lives and economy. Like most businesses in the U.S., many builders were forced to shut down operations for a period of time in 2020, reinvent processes to ensure safety, provide health training to workers, limit visits to model homes, and adapt to office staff working remotely. Builders in 2020 also had to quickly learn how to navigate the uncertainties of supply-chain disruptions that made many building materials significantly costlier and unavailable on-demand. And, as if those issues were not challenging enough, the industry's chronic labor shortage worsened as fear of the virus spread among workers and subcontractors.

Keeping this larger context in mind, table 1.2 shows that total revenue for single-family builders in 2020 averaged $13.7 million — 17% lower than the amount reported in 2017 ($16.4 million) and 16% lower than in 2014 ($16.2 million). The $13.7 million builders reported as average revenue in 2020 was 27% lower than the $18.7 million reported in 2006 (the peak in this series), but 93% higher than the $7.1 million reported in 2010 (the most recent trough).

In 2020, all costs of sales combined averaged $11.2 million, taking up 81.8% of revenue -just shy of one point higher than in 2017 (81.0%). The relative cost of land rose slightly from 12.6% of revenue to 13.0% during this period, while direct construction costs for non-single-family-building activities almost doubled from 2.6% to 5.0%. After subtracting all costs of sales from revenue, builders' average gross profit stood at $2.5 million, an 18.2% gross margin -about one point below where it stood in 2017 (19.0%). Previous editions of this study reported gross margins of 20.8% in 2006, 14.4% in 2008, 15.3% in 2010, 17.4% in 2012, and 18.9% in 2014 (see Chapter 9).

Table 1.2. Gross profit

	2014		2017		2020	
	Average ($1,000s)	Share of revenue (%)	Average ($1,000s)	Share of revenue (%)	Average ($1,000s)	Share of revenue (%)
Revenue	16,233	100.0	16,429	100.0	13,702	100.0
Cost of sales						
Land costs	2,074	12.8	2,068	12.6	1,784	13.0
Direct costs: single-family	10,014	61.7	10,306	62.7	8,242	60.1
Direct costs: multifamily, remodeling, light commercial/industrial	416	2.6	425	2.6	685	5.0
Indirect construction costs	444	2.7	469	2.9	384	2.8
Other costs*	222	1.4	42	0.3	118	0.9
Total cost of sales	13,169	81.1	13,309	81.0	11,212	81.8
Gross profit	**3,064**	**18.9**	**3,120**	**19.0**	**2,490**	**18.2**

* This category includes the costs associated with the sale of land (raw or developed), trade-ins, repossessions, rental of investment property, parking facilities, and recreational facilities, construction management activities, design activities, and other unclassified construction activities.

While the cost of sales (as a share of revenue) increased from 2017 to 2020, operating expenses shrank. After reaching an all-time low of 11.4% in 2017, these expenses hit yet a new record low in 2020, when they accounted for only 11.2% of revenue (table 1.3). For comparison, in 2008, the least profitable year in the history of this survey (the average net margin that year was -3.0%), operating expenses reached 17.4% of revenue. Rigorous belt-tightening on the part of builders has continued to cut this number down since then: to 14.7% in 2010, 12.5% in both 2012 and 2014, 11.4% in 2017, and now to 11.2% in 2020.

Looking at specific expense lines in recent years shows a steady decline in the share of revenue builders spend on sales & marketing. In 2014, builders spent 5.0% of their total revenue on this type of expense, but that share dropped to 4.7% in 2017 and then to 4.1% in 2020. Meanwhile, general & administrative expenses rose slightly from 4.1% in 2017 to 4.4% in 2020, and owner's compensation remained essentially unchanged, going from 1.2% to 1.3%. Financing expenses and depreciation were both flat during this period, at 1.3% and 0.1% of revenue, respectively.

Table 1.3. Net profit

	2014		2017		2020	
	Average ($1,000s)	Share of revenue (%)	Average ($1,000s)	Share of revenue (%)	Average ($1,000s)	Share of revenue (%)
Gross profit	3,064	18.9	3,120	19.0	2,490	18.2
Operating expenses						
Financial expenses	225	1.4	220	1.3	178	1.3
Sales & mktg. expenses	817	5.0	779	4.7	556	4.1
General & administrative expenses	766	4.7	666	4.1	597	4.4
Depreciation	n/a	n/a	19	0.1	20	0.1
Owner's compensation	215	1.3	194	1.2	180	1.3
Total operating expenes	2,023	12.5	1,879	11.4	1,531	11.2
Net profit (loss)	**1,040**	**6.4**	**1241**	**7.6**	**959**	**7.0**

In the end, tight control over operating expenses was not enough to overcome the decline in the gross profit margin in 2020, and, as a result, builders' average net margin fell slightly to 7.0% (from 7.6% in 2017). This decline comes after four consecutive increases in builders' average net profit margins in the prior four iterations of the study: from -3.0% in 2006, the average net margin went up to 0.5% in 2010, 4.9% in 2012, 6.4% in 2014, and 7.6% in 2017. The highest net profit margin ever reported in this survey was 10% in 1991. Figure 1.1 summarizes builders' income statements for 2020.

Figure 1.1. Cost of sales, expenses, and net profit (% of revenue)

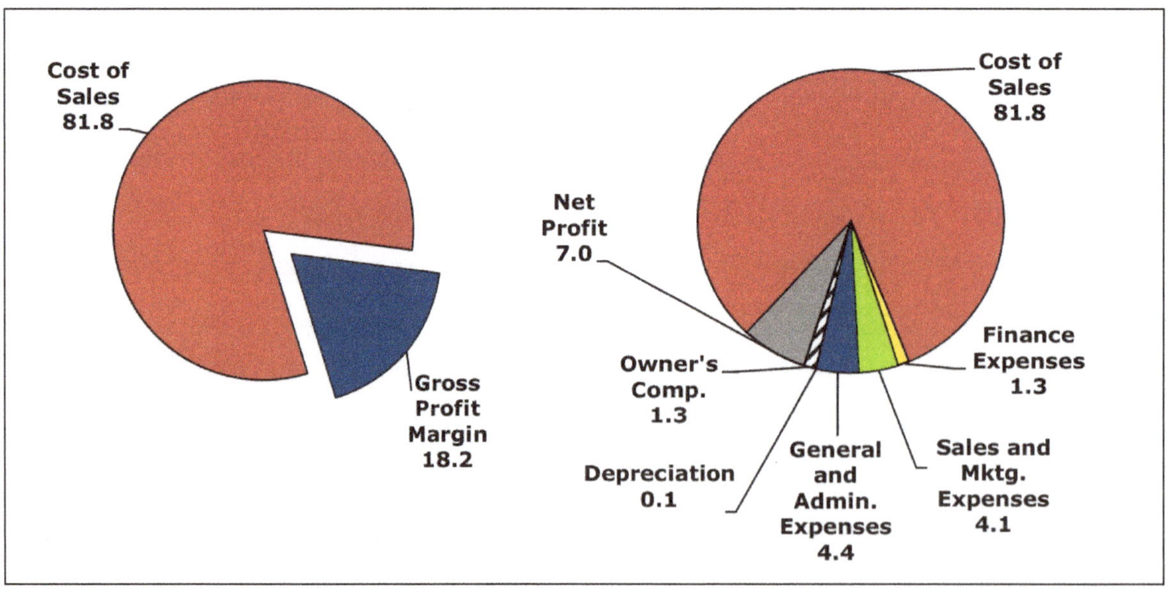

In addition to the income statement, *The Cost of Doing Business Study* has tracked the balance sheet of single-family builders over time. As table 1.4 shows, builders responding to the survey had total assets averaging $9.4 million in 2020, up 18% from 2017 ($8.0 million) and 3% from 2014 ($9.2 million)[2]. The majority of builders' assets were tied to construction work in progress ($5.9 million or 62.4% of all assets), another $850,000 was in receivables and inventories (9.0%), $571,000 in other current assets (6.0%), and $894,000 was tied to other assets (9.5%). Meanwhile, builders held an impressive average of $1.2 million in cash, representing 13.1% of all assets. In 2014 and 2017, builders only held between 7% and 8% of their assets in cash.

On the liabilities side, respondents owed an average of $6.1 million in 2020, about 15 percent more than in 2017 ($5.3 million) but 2% less than in 2014 ($6.2 million). Although the total share of assets financed through short-term liabilities has not changed significantly between 2014 (55.6%) and 2020 (55.9%), the specific type of short-term liability used is changing. While current liabilities financed 20.9% of assets in 2014, the share increased to 23.3% in 2017 and now to 30.9% in 2020. Conversely, short-term construction loans payable declined from 34.6% of assets in 2014, to 32.5% in 2017 and 24.9% in 2020.

Another balance sheet item showing declines is the share of assets financed through long-term debt: in 2014, 11.9% of assets were supported by long-term liabilities; by 2017, that share was 10.0%; and by 2020, it was 8.4%. Aggregating liabilities of all types shows that builders are relying less and less on debt to finance their operations: in 2014, 67.4% of assets were backed up by some form of debt, compared to 65.8% in 2014 and 64.3% in 2020.

In terms of the total equity builders hold in their businesses (i.e. capital investment), the amount increased to $3.4 million in 2020, up 23% from $2.7 million in 2017 and 13% from $3.0 million in 2014. This trend has pushed the share of assets financed through equity from 32.6% in 2014, to 34.2% in 2017, and now to 35.7% in 2020.

---

[2] *The Cost of Doing Business Study* is not designed as a longitudinal survey tracking the same companies over time. Instead, each year's study is based on responses from independent samples of current members of the NAHB.

Table 1.4. Balance sheet

	2014		2017		2020	
	Average ($1,000s)	Share of total (%)	Average ($1,000s)	Share of total (%)	Average ($1,000s)	Share of total (%)
Assets						
Current assets						
Cash	645	7.1	626	7.8	1,235	13.1
Receivables & inventories	n/a	n/a	588	7.3	850	9.0
Construction work in progress	6,270	68.5	5,155	64.2	5,891	62.4
Other current assets	1,274	13.9	907	11.3	571	6.0
Total current assets	8,189	89.5	7,276	90.6	8,547	90.5
Other assets	963	10.5	758	9.4	894	9.5
Total assets	**9,152**	**100.0**	**8,034**	**100.0**	**9,441**	**100.0**
Liabilities						
Current liabilities	1,917	20.9	1,869	23.3	2,921	30.9
Construction loans payable	3,169	34.6	2,611	32.5	2,356	24.9
Total current liabilities	5,086	55.6	4,480	55.8	5,276	55.9
Long-term loans payable	n/a	n/a	749	9.3	680	7.2
Other long-term liabilities	1,087	11.9	58	0.7	112	1.2
Total liabilities	**6,173**	**67.4**	**5,287**	**65.8**	**6,068**	**64.3**
Owner's equity	**2,979**	**32.6**	**2,747**	**34.2**	**3,373**	**35.7**
Total liabilities & owner's equity	**9,152**	**100.0**	**8,034**	**100.0**	**9,441**	**100.0**

The current ratio is a liquidity measure that evaluates a company's ability to repay its short-term liabilities using its short-term assets. It is calculated by dividing current assets by current liabilities, and in general, the higher the current ratio the healthier the financial state of a company. In 2020, the current ratio for all single-family home builders responding to the survey was 1.62, or in other words, builders had 62% more current assets than current liabilities. This ratio was essentially the same as in 2017 (1.62) and 2014 (1.61), but higher than in 2006 (1.43) or 2008 (1.45).

Another important gage of a company's financial health is its debt-to-equity ratio. Calculated by dividing total liabilities by total equity, this ratio measures the level of leverage, and therefore risk, that exists in a company. In 2020, builders reported an average debt-to-equity ratio of 1.80, which means builders have 80% more debt than equity in their businesses. As mentioned earlier, builders have reduced their reliance on debt to sustain their businesses in recent years, and, as result, their average debt-to-equity ratio has dropped from 2.07 in 2014, to 1.92 in 2017, and to 1.80 in 2020 (table 1.5).

As a point of reference, builders' debt-to-equity ratio reached 2.80 in 2006, a signal of the significant levels of risk taken during the housing boom. As a broader reference, a debt-to-equity ratio above 4.0 is considered so risky that most financial institutions would likely turn down additional borrowing requests from any company with that level of debt.

Two additional ratios, return on assets (ROA) and return on equity (ROE), show how effectively a company is using its assets and invested capital to churn out profits. In 2020, builders' ROA stood at 10.2%, a smaller return than in 2017 (15.4%). The decline was derived from both a lower net margin and a much higher asset position in 2020 than in 2017. Builders' ROA was still significantly higher than in 2008 (-2.7%) and 2010 (0.6%).

Similarly, significant improvements in equity paired with a lower net profit margin led builders' ROE to fall to 28.4% in 2020, down from 45.2% in 2017 and from 34.9% in 2014. Despite the drop, the 2020 ROE is still significantly higher than the ratio was in 2008 (-8.4%) or 2010 (1.9%).

Table 1.5. Financial ratios

	2014	2017	2020
Current ratio	1.61	1.62	1.62
Debt-to-equity ratio	2.07	1.92	1.80
Return on assets	11.4%	15.4%	10.2%
Return on equity	34.9%	45.2%	28.4%

Top and Bottom 25%

All businesses — and builders are no exception — continuously try to improve their operations in order to reach higher profits than just the industry average. Analyzing how the most successful quartile of builders in the study performed is therefore pivotal for understanding any builder's true competitiveness. With the latter in mind, this section shows results tabulated separately for two groups of respondents: those in the top 25% in terms of net profit margins as well as those in the bottom 25% (appendix V.2.).

Total revenue among builders in the top 25% group averaged $16.2 million in 2020, compared to only $3.7 million among the bottom 25% group. Cost of sales took up 76.3% of the former's revenue, but 90.9% of the latter's. The most dramatic dichotomy was in the share spent on direct construction costs for single-family building, since the top 25% group spent 57.4% of revenue on this cost item, compared to 70.1% among the bottom 25% group. Given such differences, the average gross profit margin was more than two times larger among the most successful group (23.7%) than among the least successful (9.1%).

At 11.3% and 11.8%, respectively, operating expenses took up similar shares of revenue among the top and bottom quartile groups. Yet the composition of those expenses varied significantly between the two. For example, the top performers spent 4.6% of revenue on sales & marketing expenses, compared to only 1.3% among the bottom performers. On the contrary, the top group spent only 1.2% on owner's compensation, compared to 3.1% among the bottom group (fig 1.2).

After subtracting operating expenses from their gross profit, the top 25% group reported an average net profit margin of 12.4%, compared to -2.7% for the bottom 25%. To put these results in historical context, since results first began to be tabulated for the top and bottom quartiles separately in 2002, the bottom 25% group has reported negative net profit margins in every study except in two years: 2014 (0.9%) and 2017 (1.1%)

Because the line between the owner's compensation and the business' profit can be blurry in many companies (especially small ones), it is useful to analyze a broader measure of performance that combines the share of revenue spent on owner's compensation and the net profit margin. As figure 1.2 shows, this overall measure of profitability was 8.3% for all builders combined, 13.6% for the top 25%, and 0.4% for the bottom 25%.

Figure 1.2. Profit margins and owner's compensation (% of revenue)

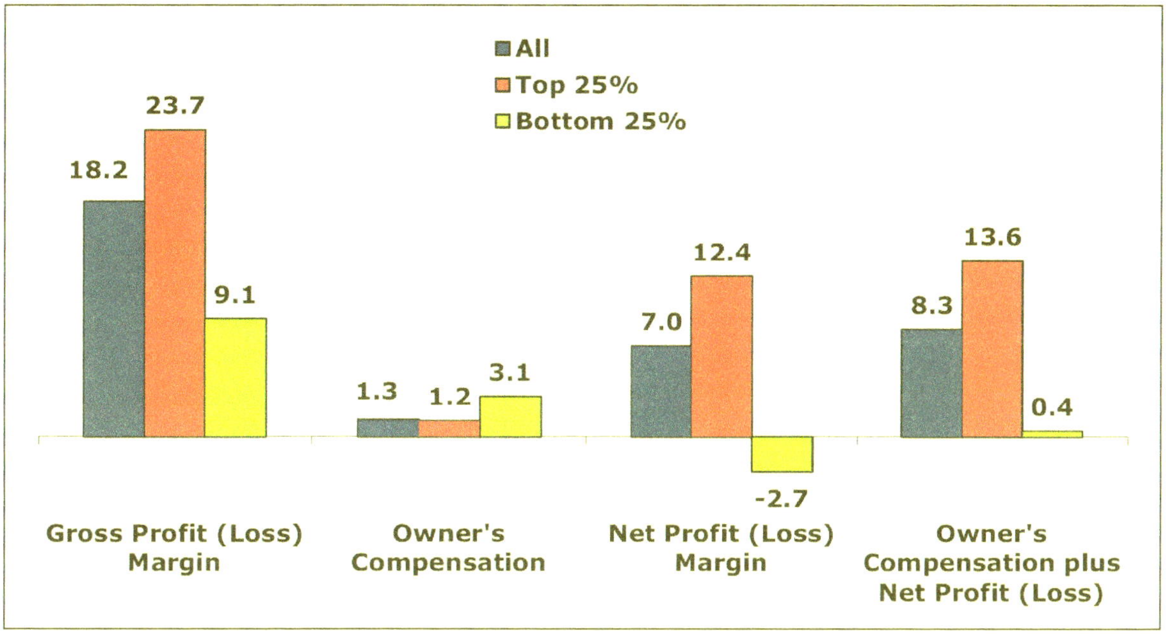

The 2020 balance sheet for the top 25% of respondents shows they had an average of $8.5 million in total assets, $5.4 million in liabilities, and $3.1 million in owner's equity. On the other hand, builders in the bottom 25% had significantly fewer assets ($2.5 million), total liabilities ($2.2 million), and owner's equity ($324,000). Table 1.6 summarizes important statistics from the income statement and balance sheet for the top and bottom 25% of respondents.

The average net profit margin among the most successful quartile of builders grew one percentage point from 11.4% in 2017 to 12.4% in 2020. Yet the group's average assets declined from $16.0 million to $8.5 million during this period, which means the 2020 cohort is made up of smaller (yet more profitable!) companies. Lower current liabilities and equity positions led this group's current ratio to improve from 1.84 in 2017 to 2.17 in 2020, but also to a slightly higher debt-to-equity ratio (1.41 to 1.72). Meanwhile, their ROE and ROA continued to grow. In 2014, this group reported a 19.3% ROA and a 33.5% ROE. In 2020, those ratios stood at 23.5% and 63.9%, respectively. That means the top performers produced revenue equivalent to about 64% of their invested capital! Compare that to interest earned when invested with lending institutions, banks or holding mortgages, and you can see what a great return they are creating.

The average net profit margin among the least successful quartile of builders, on the other hand, dipped into negative territory in 2020 (-2.7%) for the first time since the 2012 study (-4.7%). Furthermore, the group's current ratio and debt-to-equity ratio both deteriorated between 2017 and 2020: the former, from 2.29 to 1.22; the latter, from 1.39 to 6.65. Important drops in current assets and equity led to the deterioration. The ROE for the bottom 25% group of respondents was a painful -30.7% in 2020.

Table 1.6. Top and bottom 25%

	2014		2017		2020	
	Top 25%	Bottom 25%	Top 25%	Bottom 25%	Top 25%	Bottom 25%
Gross profit (loss) margin (%)	22.50	13.20	22.10	13.90	23.70	9.10
Net profit (loss) margin (%)	11.00	0.90	11.40	1.10	12.40	-2.70
Total assets (millions $)	11.75	6.87	15.97	5.63	8.54	2.48
Owner's equity (millions $)	6.76	0.50	6.61	2.36	3.10	0.32
Current ratio	2.61	1.63	1.84	2.29	2.17	1.22
Debt-to-equity ratio	0.74	12.65	1.41	1.39	1.72	6.65
Return on assets (%)	19.30	1.00	21.10	1.50	23.50	-4.00
Return on equity (%)	33.50	13.80	50.80	3.50	63.90	-30.70

2

Builders With Land Costs

Builders with land costs (those that only build spec or presold homes on their own lots) responding to *The Cost of Doing Business Study* averaged $14.2 million in total revenue in 2020, about 3% lower than in 2017 ($14.7) and 31% lower than in 2014 ($20.5 million) (table 2.1). Builders with land costs spent a larger share of revenue on costs of sales items in 2020 (80.7%) than in 2017 (79.1%), but less than in 2014 (81.6%). The most important change in the cost structure since the last study was the increase in the share of revenue spent on direct construction costs (i.e. construction labor, material, and subcontractors) to build single-family homes, which rose from 55.0% to 58.9%. On average, builders with land costs reported a 19.3% gross profit margin in 2020 ($2.7 million), the third largest in the series for this group after 2006 (22.1%) and 2017 (20.9%).

Among the three types of business models analyzed in this study *builders with land costs, builders without land costs,* and *combination builders* those with land costs achieved the highest gross profit margin in 2020, at 19.3%. In contrast, the average gross margin was 13.2% among builders without land costs and 17.7% among combination builders (Appendix V.1.).

Table 2.1. Gross profit

	2014		2017		2020	
	Average ($1,000s)	**Share of revenue (%)**	**Average ($1,000s)**	**Share of revenue (%)**	**Average ($1,000s)**	**Share of revenue (%)**
Revenue	20,453	100.0	14,726	100.0	14,214	100.0
Cost of sales						
Land costs	3,275	16.0	2,547	17.3	2,523	17.8
Direct costs: single-family	12,132	59.3	8,103	55.0	8,378	58.9
Direct costs: multifamily, remodeling, light commercial/industrial	301	1.5	629	4.3	30	0.2
Indirect construction costs	527	2.6	363	2.5	537	3.8
Other costs	458	2.2	10	0.1	9	0.1
Total cost of sales	16,694	81.6	11,652	79.1	11,476	80.7
Gross profit	**3,758**	**18.4**	**3,074**	**20.9**	**2,738**	**19.3**

On a net basis, builders with land costs lost money in fiscal years 2008 (-4.9%) and 2010 (-1.0%), in large part due to running their businesses with operating expenses that exceeded 18% of their total revenue. Years later, after reigning in and lowering all these expenses to 10.6% in 2017, they achieved an impressive 10.3% net profit margin (table 2.2). In 2020, however, operating expenses regained strength, and their share of revenue rose to 12.6%. The increase was led by higher general and administrative expenses, which went from accounting for 3.4% of revenue in 2017 to 4.8% in 2020.

In the end, builders with land costs posted an average net profit of $943,000 in fiscal year 2020, for a net margin of 6.6%. That was the third most profitable year for builders with land costs in the history of the study, after 2006 (9.1%) and 2017 (10.3%). Figure 2.1 summarizes the income statement for builders with land costs for 2020.

Table 2.2. Net profit

	2014		2017		2020	
	Average ($1,000s)	Share of revenue (%)	Average ($1,000s)	Share of revenue (%)	Average ($1,000s)	Share of revenue (%)
Gross profit	3,758	18.4	3,074	20.9	2,738	19.3
Operating expenses						
Financing expenses	393	1.9	233	1.6	253	1.8
Sales & mktg. expenses	1,012	4.9	670	4.5	744	5.2
General & administrative expenses	849	4.2	493	3.4	678	4.8
Depreciation	n/a	n/a	11	0.1	6	0.0
Owner's compensation	299	1.5	153	1.0	115	0.8
Total operating expenses	2,552	12.5	1,559	10.6	1,795	12.6
Net profit (loss)	**1,206**	**5.9**	**1,514**	**10.3**	**943**	**6.6**

Figure 2.1. Cost of sales, expenses, and net profit (% of revenue)

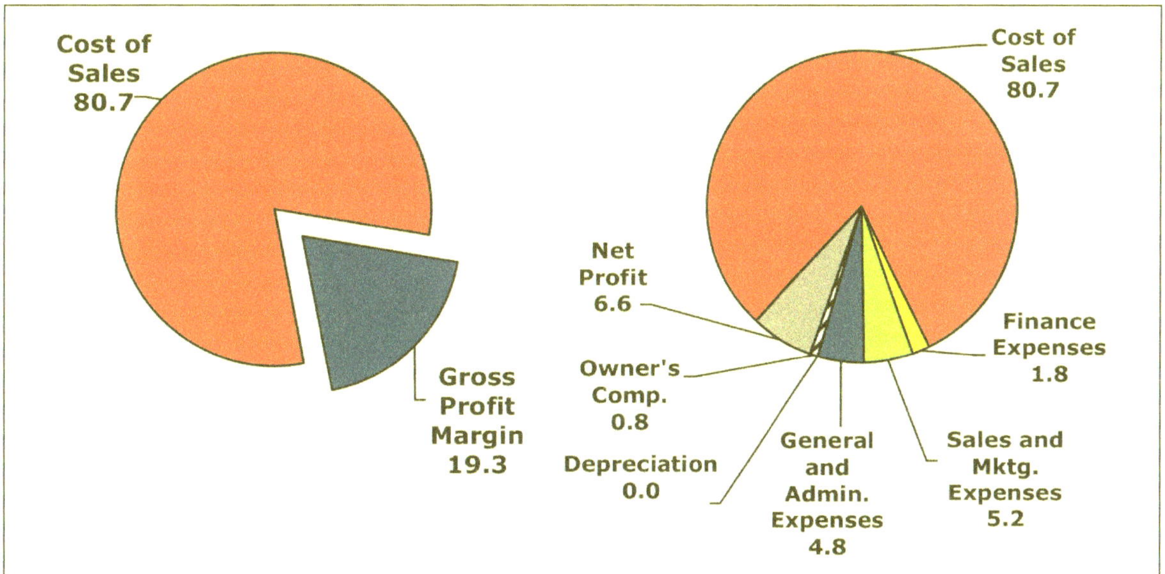

The balance sheet for the average builder with land costs was larger in 2020 ($9.5 million in assets) than in 2017 ($8.6 million), but smaller than in 2014 ($13.6 million). Close analysis of the latest data shows strong growth in two specific types of assets since 2017. That year, builders with land costs held an average 8.0% of their assets ($686,000) in cash; by 2020, that share was up to 12.6% ($1.2 million). Similarly, construction work in progress rose from 61.2% ($5.3 million) to 69.2% ($6.5 million) of assets during this period.

In addition, this group of builders reported an average of $451,000 (4.8% of assets) in accounts receivables and inventories in 2020 and $453,000 (4.8%) in other current assets (such as refundable deposits and furnished model homes). All combined, this group's current assets accounted for 91.3% of total assets – higher than in 2017 (84.4%) and 2014 (88.7 %) (table 2.3).

On the liabilities' side of the ledger, current liabilities increased substantially for builders with land costs from 2017 to 2020, going from 12.1% of assets ($1.0 million) to 31.5% ($2.9 million). As a result, they ended fiscal year 2020 with $6.5 million in total debt (69.0% of assets), about 18% more than in 2017 ($5.6 million). Higher levels of debt meant this group of builders relied less heavily on their own invested capital to finance their operations. On average, owner's equity in 2020 supported 31.0% of their assets, down from 35.6% in 2017.

Table 2.3. Balance sheet

	2014		2017		2020	
	Average ($1,000s)	Share of total (%)	Average ($1,000s)	Share of total (%)	Average ($1,000s)	Share of total (%)
Assets						
Current assets						
Cash	955	7.0	686	8.0	1,189	12.6
Receivables & Inventories	n/a	n/a	674	7.8	451	4.8
Construction work in progress	9,109	67.0	5,282	61.2	6,546	69.2
Other current assets	1,994	14.7	636	7.4	453	4.8
Total current assets	12,057	88.7	7,278	84.4	8,640	91.3
Other assets	1,538	11.3	1,350	15.6	823	8.7
Total assets	**13,594**	**100.0**	**8,628**	**100.0**	**9,463**	**100.0**
Liabilities						
Current liabilities	2,826	20.8	1,042	12.1	2,985	31.5
Construction loans payable	5,010	36.9	3,393	39.3	2,344	24.8
Total current liabilities	7,835	57.6	4,434	51.4	5,329	56.3
Long-term loans payable	n/a	n/a	1,010	11.7	1,117	11.8
Other long-term liabilities	2,372	17.4	108	1.3	80	0.8
Total liabilities	10,207	75.1	5,553	64.4	6,525	69.0
Owner's equity	3,387	24.9	3,075	35.6	2,938	31.0
Total liabilities & owner's equity	13,594	100.0	8,628	100.0	9,463	100.0

Since both current assets and current liabilities rose in 2020 for builders with land costs, their average current ratio changed little (1.62) from 2017 (1.64). On the other hand, the debt-to-equity ratio increased from 1.81 to 2.22, driven by the higher debt levels and lower equity position described above. This implies builders with land costs held 2.22 times more debt than equity in 2020. In sum, a lower profit margin and shifts in the composition of balance sheets led to decreases in these builders' ROA (17.6% to 10.0%) and ROE (49.2% to 32.1%) from 2017 to 2020 (table 2.4).

Table 2.4. Financial ratios

	2014	2017	2020
Current ratio	1.54	1.64	1.62
Debt-to-equity ratio	3.01	1.81	2.22
Return on assets (%)	8.90	17.6	10.0
Return on equity (%)	35.60	49.2	32.1

Note: No data for the top and bottom 25% of builders with land costs were produced because of insufficient sample size.

3

Builders Without Land Costs

Builders without land costs (those that build exclusively on their customers' land) brought in an all-time high $8.7 million in revenue in 2020. That was 43% more than the previous series peak of $6.1 million reported in 2017 (table 3.1). The substantial increase in revenue was driven primarily by strong gains from residential remodeling, light commercial, and multifamily building. Combined, these activities brought builders without land costs an average $2.5 million in revenue in 2020, up from only $231,000 in 2017.

Not surprisingly, a much larger share of revenue was spent on direct construction costs for residential remodeling, light commercial, and multifamily building in 2020 (24.1%) than in 2017 (3.0%). Altogether, cost of sales took up $7.5 million, or 86.8% of all revenue in 2020, which left this group of builders with an average gross profit of $1.1 million — a 13.2% gross profit margin. That margin was two whole points lower than in 2017 (15.3%) and just slightly lower than in 2014 (13.6%).

Table 3.1. Gross profit

	2014		2017		2020	
	Average ($1,000s)	Share of revenue (%)	Average ($1,000s)	Share of revenue (%)	Average ($1,000s)	Share of revenue (%)
Revenue	4,931	100.0	6,076	100.0	8,692	100.0
Cost of sales						
Land costs	0	0.0	0	0.0	0	0.0
Direct costs: single-family	3,276	66.4	4,787	78.8	5,414	62.3
Direct costs: multifamily, remodeling, light commercial/industrial	624	12.7	184	3.0	2,091	24.1
Indirect construction costs	167	3.4	103	1.7	43	0.5
Other costs	191	3.9	72	1.2	0	0.0
Total cost of sales	4,258	86.4	5,145	84.7	7,548	86.8
Gross profit	**673**	**13.6**	**931**	**15.3**	**1,143**	**13.2**

Quite impressively, however, the share of revenue builders without land costs spent on operating expenses declined by 2.5 percentage points from 2017 to 2020, going from 11.1% to 8.6% (table 3.2). The belt-tightening took place mostly around general and administrative expenses, which went from accounting for 7.0% of revenue to only 4.6%. Such significant reductions in expenses allowed builders without land costs to end fiscal year 2020 with an average net profit of $395,000, about 53% higher than in 2017 ($258,000). That translated into an average net profit margin of 4.5% — the second-best net margin for builders without land costs behind 2008's 5.1%. Figure 3.1 summarizes the income statement for builders without land costs for 2020.

Table 3.2. Net profit

	2014		2017		2020	
	Average ($1,000s)	Share of revenue (%)	Average ($1,000s)	Share of revenue (%)	Average ($1,000s)	Share of revenue (%)
Gross profit	673	13.6	931	15.3	1,143	13.2
Operating expenses						
Financing expenses	7	0.2	7	0.1	3	0.0
Sales & mktg. expenses	34	0.7	38	0.6	27	0.3
General & administrative expenses	314	6.4	426	7.0	396	4.6
Depreciation	n/a	n/a	11	0.2	22	0.2
Owner's compensation	141	2.9	191	3.1	301	3.5
Total operating expenses	496	10.2	673	11.1	748	8.6
Net profit (loss)	**176**	**3.6**	**258**	**4.3**	**395**	**4.5**

Figure 3.1 Cost of sales, expenses, and net profit (% of revenue)

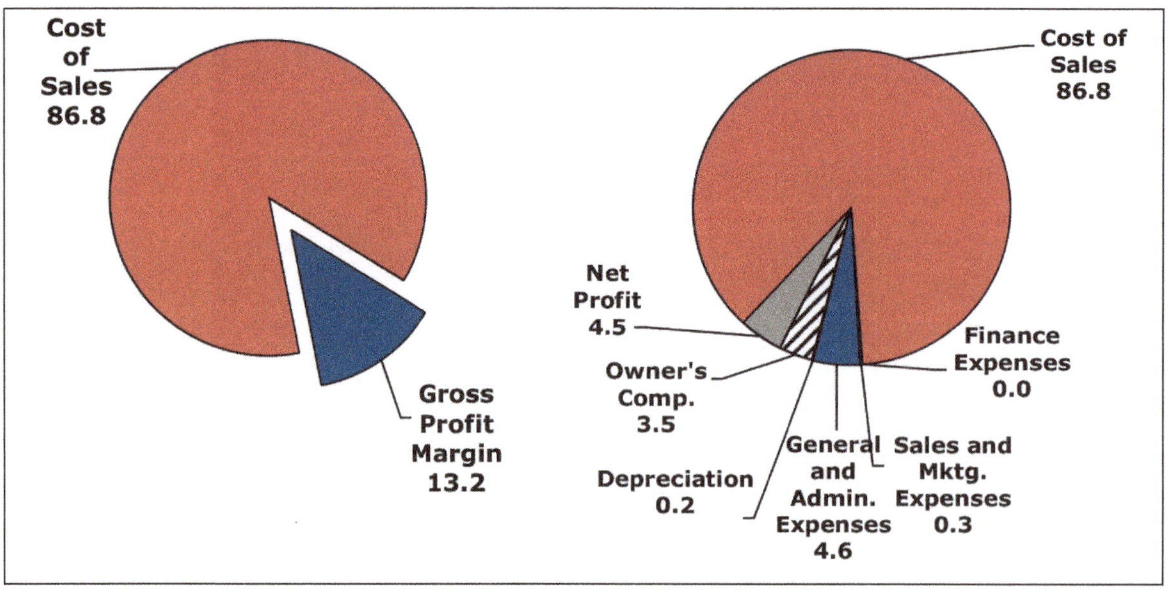

Looking at their balance sheets, it is clear the cohort of builders without land costs responding to the 2020 study is made up of significantly larger companies than in the past. In 2020, this group of builders reported an average of $5.4 million in total assets, nearly four times the $1.4 million average in 2017. The most dramatic difference was in the amount of assets held as construction work in progress, which skyrocketed to $4.3 million (80.7% of all assets.), 10 times the average in 2017 ($432,000). Cash, on the other hand, only accounted for 5.5% of their assets. Overall, 97.3% of all the assets held by this group of builders were current, up from 90.8% in 2017 and 81.2% in 2014 (table 3.3).

In order to finance the steep increase in assets, builders without land costs substantially increased the capital invested in their own companies. In 2020, their balance sheets showed an average of $3.9 million in equity, up from $685,000 in 2017. As a result, the share of all assets financed through equity rose from 50.6% to 72.2% during this period. On the contrary, although average liabilities doubled from $668,000 in 2017 to $1.5 million in 2020, the share of assets financed through debt dropped from 49.4% to 27.8%.

Table 3.3. Balance sheet

	2014		2017		2020	
	Average ($1,000s)	Share of total (%)	Average ($1,000s)	Share of total (%)	Average ($1,000s)	Share of total (%)
Assets						
Current assets						
Cash	214	16.3	307	22.7	294	5.5
Receivables and Inventories	n/a	n/a	441	32.6	464	8.6
Construction work in progress	451	34.3	432	31.9	4,344	80.7
Other current assets	403	30.6	48	3.6	133	2.5
Total current assets	1,068	81.2	1,229	90.8	5,235	97.3
Other assets	248	18.8	125	9.2	148	2.7
Total assets	**1,316**	**100.0**	**1,353**	**100.0**	**5,383**	**100.0**
Liabilities						
Current liabilities	744	56.5	559	41.3	1,433	26.6
Construction loans payable	32	2.5	71	5.3	4	0.1
Total current liabilities	777	59.0	630	46.5	1,437	26.7
Long-term loans payable	n/a	n/a	23	1.7	58	1.1
Other long-term liabilities	204	15.5	15	1.1	3	0.1
Total liabilities	**980**	**74.5**	**668**	**49.4**	**1,499**	**27.8**
Owner's equity	**335**	**25.5**	**685**	**50.6**	**3,884**	**72.2**
Total liabilities & owner's equity	**1,316**	**100.0**	**1,353**	**100.0**	**5,383**	**100.0**

Financial ratios for builders without land costs reveal these builders have become increasingly risk-averse in recent years. Much higher levels of current assets in 2020 drove their current ratio up to 3.64, far above 2017 (1.95) or 2014 (1.38), and the highest it has been since 2010 (3.69). Moreover, substantial injections of capital into their businesses continued to drive down the debt-to-equity ratio (a measure of risk), which has fallen from 2.92 in 2014, to 0.97 in 2017, and now to 0.39 in 2020 (table 3.4).

Higher absolute levels of assets or equity, however, do not necessarily translate into higher returns on assets or returns on equity if net profit margins do not grow proportionally. This is precisely what happened to builders without land costs between 2017 and 2020, who saw their ROA drop from 19.1% to 7.3% and their ROE from 37.7% to 10.2% during this period. These levels should be considered too low given the risks related to building on other people's property.

Table 3.4. Financial ratios

	2014	2017	2020
Current ratio	1.38	1.95	3.64
Debt-to-equity ratio	2.92	0.97	0.39
Return on assets (%)	13.40	19.1	7.3
Return on equity (%)	52.60	37.7	10.2

Note: No data for the top and bottom 25% of builders without land costs were produced because of insufficient sample size.

4

Combination Builders

In this study, combination builders are defined as those who build homes both on their own land and on land owned by their customers. This hybrid group of builders averaged $15.2 million in total revenue during 2020, which was 24% lower than in 2017 ($19.9 million), but essentially unchanged from 2014 ($15.4 million) (table 4.1). Comparing cost structures from 2017 to 2020 shows the share of revenue spent on direct construction costs to build single-family homes declined from 67.0% to 63.8%, while the share spent on direct costs for remodeling, multifamily, and light commercial rose from 1.9% to 5.3%. Relative to revenue, land costs remained rather constant, just above 10.0%. Added together, all items under costs of sales took up 82.3% of the total revenue combination builders generated in 2020, leaving them with a gross profit margin of 17.7%. That was slightly ahead of their gross margin in 2017 (17.2%), but about two points lower than in 2014 (19.5%). In absolute dollar terms, combination builders posted an average gross profit of $2.7 million, 22% lower than in 2017 ($3.4 million) and 11% lower than in 2014 ($3.0 million).

Table 4.1. Gross profit

	2014		2017		2020	
	Average ($1,000s)	Share of revenue (%)	Average ($1,000s)	Share of revenue (%)	Average ($1,000s)	Share of revenue (%)
Revenue	15,437	100.0	19,917	100.0	15,211	100.0
Cost of sales						
Land costs	2,143	13.9	2,060	10.3	1,603	10.5
Direct costs: single-family	9,337	60.5	13,344	67.0	9,707	63.8
Direct costs: multifamily, remodeling, light commercial/industrial	423	2.7	380	1.9	804	5.3
Indirect construction costs	472	3.1	641	3.2	399	2.6
Other costs	48	0.3	59	0.3	5	0.0
Total cost of sales	12,424	80.5	16,483	82.8	12,519	82.3
Gross profit	**3,013**	**19.5**	**3,434**	**17.2**	**2,692**	**17.7**

In both 2014 and 2017, combination builders spent 11.9% of their revenue paying for operating expenses. In 2020, however, they managed to drive these expenses down to only 10.5% of revenue. The most important reduction came in sales and marketing expenses, which dropped from 5.2% of revenue to only 3.8%. General and administrative expenses also declined, but to a lesser extent (4.5% to 3.9%). After subtracting all expenses, combination builders posted an average net profit of $1.1 million in 2020, a 7.2% net profit margin. That was the second highest net profit margin in the history of the series for combination builders, after the 7.6% reported in 2014 (table 4.2). Figure 4.1 summarizes the income statement for combination builders for 2020.

Among the three business models analyzed in this study, combination builders had the highest net profit margin in 2020, at 7.2%. Builders with land costs followed in second place, with a net margin of 6.6%. The lowest average net margin in 2020 belonged to builders without land costs, at 4.5% (Appendix V.1.).

Table 4.2. Net profit

	2014		2017		2020	
	Average ($1,000s)	Share of revenue (%)	Average ($1,000s)	Share of revenue (%)	Average ($1,000s)	Share of revenue (%)
Gross profit	3,013	19.5	3,434	17.2	2,692	17.7
Operating expenses						
Financing expenses	204	1.3	228	1.1	186	1.2
Sales & mktg. expenses	806	5.2	1,027	5.2	576	3.8
General & administrative expenses	644	4.2	901	4.5	589	3.9
Depreciation	n/a	n/a	28	0.1	33	0.2
Owner's compensation	184	1.2	186	0.9	206	1.4
Total operating expenses	1,838	11.9	2,370	11.9	1,590	10.5
Net profit (loss)	**1,175**	**7.6**	**1,064**	**5.3**	**1,102**	**7.2**

Figure 4.1. Cost of sales, expenses, and net profit (% of revenue)

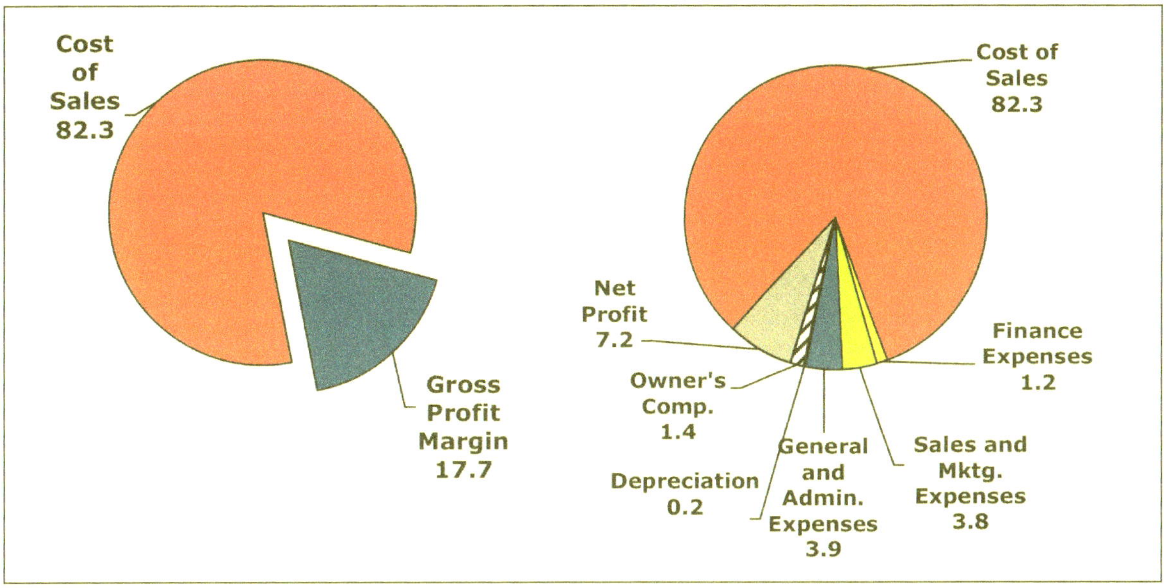

The average 2020 balance sheet among combination builders showed assets totaling $9.3 million, up about 9% from $8.5 million in 2017 and about the same as in 2014 ($9.4 million). Some types of assets increased significantly from 2017 to 2020. Cash, for example, went from accounting for 5.5% ($469,000) of all assets to 14.0% ($1.3 million). Receivables and inventories rose from 6.8% ($583,000) to 12.4% ($1.2 million). On the other hand, construction work in progress went from representing 73.6% ($6.3 million) of all assets to 57.4% ($5.4 million). All combined, this group's current assets accounted for 90.7% of assets, down slightly from 92.9% in 2017 (table 4.3).

Combination builders financed the recent increase in total assets by investing or retaining more of their own capital rather than by taking out new loans. In 2017, current liabilities backed up 64.1% of their assets; by 2020, that share had dropped to 53.7%. In all, total debt (current plus long-term) averaged $5.9 million (62.8% of assets) in 2020, down from $6.0 million (70.7% of assets) in 2017. On the contrary, combination builders held more equity in 2020 (an average of $3.5 million) than in 2017 ($2.5 million). As a result, the share of their assets financed through equity rose from 29.3% to 37.2% during this period.

Table 4.3. Balance sheet

	2014		2017		2020	
	Average ($1,000s)	Share of total (%)	Average ($1,000s)	Share of total (%)	Average ($1,000s)	Share of total (%)
Assets						
Current assets						
Cash	592	6.3	469	5.5	1,307	14.0
Receivables and inventories	n/a	n/a	583	6.8	1,158	12.4
Construction work in progress	6,954	74.2	6,279	73.6	5,355	57.4
Other current assets	1,155	12.3	589	6.9	630	6.8
Total current assets	8,701	92.8	7,920	92.9	8,450	90.7
Other assets	676	7.2	608	7.1	871	9.3
Total assets	9,377	100.0	8,528	100.0	9,321	100.0
Liabilities						
Current liabilities	1,579	16.8	3,050	35.8	2,656	28.5
Construction loans payable	3,493	37.3	2,414	28.3	2,352	25.2
Total current liabilities	5,072	54.1	5,464	64.1	5,008	53.7
Long-term loans payable	n/a	n/a	526	6.2	634	6.8
Other long-term liabilities	569	6.1	40	0.5	209	2.2
Total liabilities	**5,641**	**60.2**	**6,031**	**70.7**	**5,851**	**62.8**
Owner's equity	**3,736**	**39.8**	**2,497**	**29.3**	**3,470**	**37.2**
Total liabilities & owner's equity	**9,377**	**100.0**	**8,528**	**100.0**	**9,321**	**100.0**

Simultaneously increasing assets and holding down debt allowed combination builders to improve some financial ratios. The current ratio, for example, rose from 1.45 in 2017 to 1.69 in 2020, signaling a higher level of liquidity in these companies. At the same time, their debt-to-equity ratio dropped from 2.42 in 2017 to 1.69 in 2020, indicating lower levels of risk and deleveraging (table 4.4).

Nonetheless, the strong gains in both assets and equity without a proportional increase in net profits led to some deterioration in this group's ROA and ROE (although both remained in positive territory). The former slipped from 12.5% in 2017 to 11.8% in 2020, while the latter fell from 42.6% to 31.8%.

Table 4.4. Financial ratios

	2014	2017	2020
Current ratio	1.72	1.45	1.69
Debt-to-equity ratio	1.51	2.42	1.69
Return on assets (%)	12.50	12.50	11.80
Return on equity (%)	31.40	42.60	31.80

Note: No data for the top and bottom 25% of combination builders were produced because of insufficient sample size.

5

Small-Volume Builders

All Small-Volume Builders Combined

A small-volume builder, as defined in this study, is one that closes 25 or fewer units per year. According to the 2020 NAHB Builder Member Census, approximately 83% of our association's single-family builders fall under this classification. Total revenue for the typical small-volume builder in 2020 was $5.4 million, about 23% higher than in 2017 ($4.4 million) and 17% more than in 2014 ($4.6 million). Most of the increase in revenue from 2017 to 2020 stemmed from residential remodeling and light commercial building, which explains the sharp increase in the share of revenue spent on direct construction costs for these activities during this period, up from 4.9% to 12.9%. Altogether, costs of sales totaled $4.7 million in 2020, or 86.4% of all revenue — a higher share than in 2017 (83.2%). That left small builders with a gross profit of $740,000, a 13.6% gross margin — around three points lower than in 2017 (16.8%) or 2014 (16.4%) (table 5.1).

Table 5.1. Gross profit

	2014		2017		2020	
	Average ($1,000s)	**Share of revenue (%)**	**Average ($1,000s)**	**Share of revenue (%)**	**Average ($1,000s)**	**Share of revenue (%)**
Revenue	4,628	100.0	4,400	100.0	5,432	100.0
Cost of Sales						
Land costs	277	6.0	347	7.9	335	6.2
Direct costs: single-family	2,899	62.6	2,973	67.6	3,546	65.3
Direct costs: multifamily, remodeling, light commercial/industrial	459	9.9	217	4.9	702	12.9
Indirect construction costs	129	2.8	119	2.7	106	1.9
Other costs	106	2.3	6	0.1	4	0.1
Total cost of Sales	3,871	83.6	3,662	83.2	4,693	86.4
Gross profit	**757**	**16.4**	**737**	**16.8**	**740**	**13.6**

Small-volume builders spent an average of $533,000 on operating expenses in 2020. Nearly half of that amount paid for general and administrative expenses ($244,000 or 4.5% of revenue), followed by compensation to the owner ($165,000 or 3.0% of revenue). As a share of revenue, however, all operating expenses combined declined from 2017 to 2020, 11.0% to 9.8%.

Yet in the end, all that belt-tightening was not enough to make up for the deterioration in their gross profit margin. Despite the relatively lower operating expenses, small builders posted a lower net profit margin in 2020 (3.8%) than in 2017 (5.7%) (table 5.2). The decline reverses a decade-long trend of rising net margins for small builders, which after sinking to -1.4% in 2008, went on to increase in 2010 (1.9%), 2012 (4.0%), 2014 (5.0%), and 2017 (5.7% — the peak in this group's history). Figure 5.1 summarizes the income statement for small-volume builders for 2020 (Appendix V.3.).

Table 5.2. Net profit

	2014		2017		2020	
	Average ($1,000s)	**Share of revenue (%)**	**Average ($1,000s)**	**Share of revenue (%)**	**Average ($1,000s)**	**Share of revenue (%)**
Gross profit	757	16.4	737	16.8	740	13.6
Operating expenses						
Financing expenses	40	0.9	30	0.7	39	0.7
Sales & mktg. expenses	92	2.0	104	2.4	73	1.3
General & administrative expenses	268	5.8	229	5.2	244	4.5
Depreciation	n/a	n/a	5	0.1	12	0.2
Owner's compensation	125	2.7	118	2.7	165	3.0
Total operating expenses	525	11.3	486	11.0	533	9.8
Net profit (loss)	**232**	**5.0**	**251**	**5.7**	**207**	**3.8**

Figure 5.1. Cost of sales, expenses, and net profit (% of revenue)

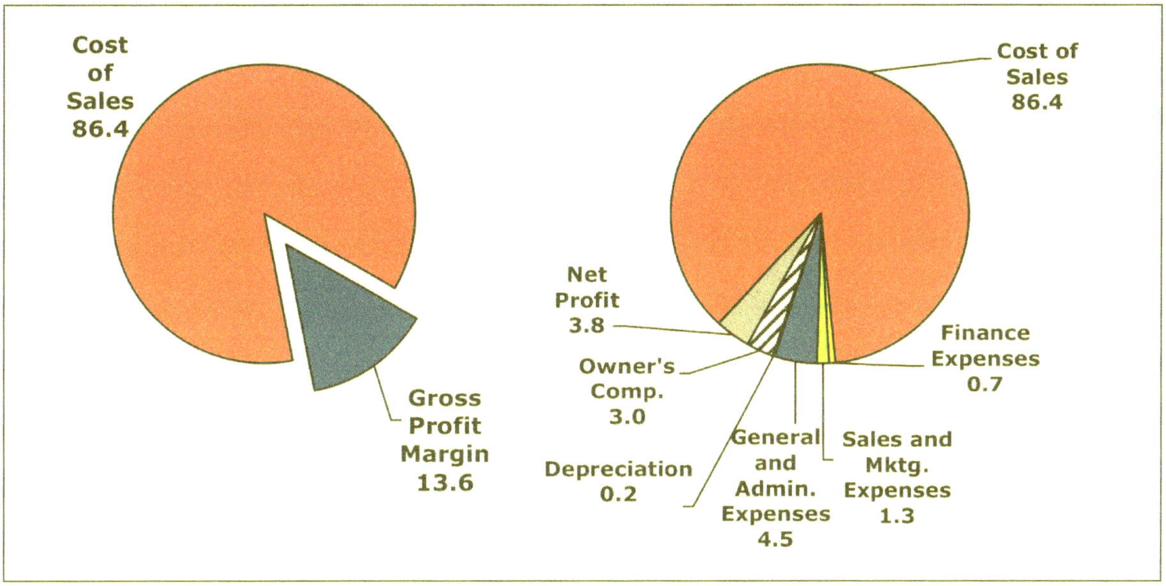

In terms of their balance sheets, small-volume builders doubled the size of their assets. Their ledgers show an average of $3.6 million in total assets in 2020, up from $1.8 million in 2017 – a 103% increase! The composition of those assets changed dramatically during this period. For example, construction work in progress went from accounting for 34.2% of assets in 2017 to 71.1% in 2020. At the same time, receivables and inventory fell from 20.0% to 8.5%. Together, all forms of current assets represented 96.9% of total assets (up from 72.3% in 2017), which means only a tiny 3.1% of assets were fixed (down from 27.7% in 2017) (table 5.3).

The other side of the ledgers show that small builders financed the increase in assets primarily by taking out more debt, but also (to a lesser extent) by investing or retaining more of their own money and profits. From 2017 to 2020, current liabilities jumped from $615,000 (34.3% of assets) to $1.8 million (49.9%), leading to a 152% increase in overall debt ($770,000 to $1.9 million). As a result, the share of assets supported by liabilities increased from 42.9% to 53.5%. During this period, small builders also increased their average invested capital ($1.0 million to $1.7 million), yet equity financed a smaller portion of assets in 2020 (46.5%) than in 2017 (57.1%).

Table 5.3. Balance sheet

	2014		2017		2020	
	Average ($1,000s)	Share of total (%)	Average ($1,000s)	Share of total (%)	Average ($1,000s)	Share of total (%)
Assets						
Current assets						
Cash	297	12.7	218	12.2	351	9.7
Receivables and Inventories	n/a	n/a	358	20.0	309	8.5
Construction work in Progress	1,195	50.9	613	34.2	2,583	71.1
Other current assets	469	20.0	107	6.0	278	7.6
Total current assets	1,961	83.6	1,296	72.3	3,521	96.9
Other assets	385	16.4	497	27.7	112	3.1
Total assets	**2,346**	**100.0**	**1,794**	**100.0**	**3,633**	**100.0**
Liabilities						
Current liabilities	616	26.3	392	21.8	951	26.2
Construction loans Payable	699	29.8	224	12.5	863	23.7
Total current liabilities	1,315	56.1	615	34.3	1,814	49.9
Long-term loans payable	n/a	n/a	84	4.7	95	2.6
Other long-term liabilities	325	13.9	71	3.9	33	0.9
Total liabilities	**1,640**	**69.9**	**770**	**42.9**	**1,942**	**53.5**
Owner's equity	**706**	**30.1**	**1,024**	**57.1**	**1,691**	**46.5**
Total liabilities & owner's equity	**2,346**	**100.0**	**1,794**	**100.0**	**3,633**	**100.0**

The combination of lower net profits and significantly higher levels of debt caused some deterioration in the financial health of the typical small-volume builder, demonstrated by changes in this group's financial ratios. The current ratio, for example, dropped to 1.94 in 2020, down from 2.11 in 2017. This means small builders are somewhat less able to cover their immediate debts with the amount of liquid assets they hold (but still have plenty of working capital as a reading over 1.4 is good).

Not surprisingly, the debt-to-equity ratio rose to 1.15 in 2020, up from 0.75 in 2017 — a clear illustration of small builders' heightened reliance on debt to run their businesses during this period. In the end, lower returns coupled with higher levels of assets and equity caused a steep decline in this group's ROA and ROE. Return on assets fell from 14.0% in 2017 to 5.7% in 2020, while return on equity was cut in half, from 24.5% to 12.2%

(table 5.4). This also represents a poor return relative to the risks of the construction business and could indicate an opportunity to reduce equity via draws, distributions and/or dividends, which would drive up the returns. As a side result, there is less money for would-be lawsuits to entangle the company and possibly tap into.

Table 5.4. Financial ratios

	2014	2017	2020
Current ratio	1.49	2.11	1.94
Debt-to-equity ratio	2.32	0.75	1.15
Return on assets (%)	9.90	14.00	5.70
Return on equity (%)	32.80	24.50	12.20

Small-Volume Builders with Land Costs

In order to provide builders reading this study the ability to compare their financial performance against their closest peers, the rest of this chapter breaks down small-volume builders into two different subsets. This first section analyzes the performance of small-volume builders with land costs, in other words, builders with 25 or fewer closings a year who only build spec or pre-sold homes on their own lots. The following section will analyze the performance of combination small-volume builders, who also have 25 or fewer closings, but build both on their land as well as on their customers' land.

After rising steadily for the past decade, average revenue among small builders with land costs declined to $3.2 million in 2020, down 21% from 2017 ($4.0 million) and 9% from 2014 ($3.5 million). The last year in this series in which revenue for this subset of builders was lower than in 2020 was 2012, when it averaged $2.9 million.

Land costs remained relatively unchanged from 2017 (19.7% of revenue) to 2020 (20.2%), but quite the opposite is true of the direct costs involved with building single-family homes, which skyrocketed from 51.9% of revenue to 63.2% (this line includes the cost of direct labor, materials, and subcontractors). Altogether, cost of sales took up a staggering 89.3% of all revenue, leaving small builders with land costs with an average gross profit margin of only 10.7% ($340,000). That gross margin was 10 points lower than in 2017 (20.8%) and 13 points lower than in 2014 (23.6%) (table 5.5).

Table 5.5. Small-volume builders with land costs: gross profit

	2014		2017		2020	
	Average ($1,000s)	Share of revenue (%)	Average ($1,000s)	Share of revenue (%)	Average ($1,000s)	Share of revenue (%)
Revenue	3,467	100.0	3,997	100.0	3,168	100.0
Cost of sales						
Land costs	553	16.0	788	19.7	641	20.2
Direct costs: single-family	1,844	53.2	2,076	51.9	2,003	63.2
Direct costs: multifamily, remodeling, light commercial/industrial	147	4.2	204	5.1	49	1.5
Indirect construction costs	95	2.7	99	2.5	127	4.0
Other costs	9	0.3	0	0.0	8	0.3
Total cost of sales	2,647	76.4	3,167	79.2	2,828	89.3
Gross profit	**820**	**23.6**	**830**	**20.8**	**340**	**10.7**

Small-volume builders with land costs managed to significantly reduce their operating expenses in 2020, likely driven by the need to make up for the collapse of their gross margin. In all, operating expenses took up only 9.6% of revenue, compared to 12.5% in 2017. Even the average compensation paid to owners declined during this period, from $93,000 to $82,000 (table 5.6). In the end, their net profit averaged only $34,000, a net margin of barely 1.1% — the lowest in this series since 2010 (0.7%). Figure 5.2 summarizes the income statement for small-volume builders with land costs for 2020 (Appendix V.4.).

Table 5.6. Small-volume builders with land costs: net profit

	2014		2017		2020	
	Average ($1,000s)	Share of revenue (%)	Average ($1,000s)	Share of revenue (%)	Average ($1,000s)	Share of revenue (%)
Gross profit	820	23.6	830	20.8	340	10.7
Operating expenses						
Financing expenses	64	1.8	64	1.6	66	2.1
Sales & mktg. expenses	168	4.8	175	4.4	76	2.4
General & administrative expenses	170	4.9	165	4.1	79	2.5
Depreciation	n/a	n/a	2	0.1	3	0.1
Owner's compensation	123	3.6	93	2.3	82	2.6
Total operating expenses	525	15.1	500	12.5	305	9.6
Net profit (loss)	**295**	**8.5**	**330**	**8.3**	**34**	**1.1**

Figure 5.2. Small-volume builders with land costs: cost of sales, expenses, and net profit (% of revenue)

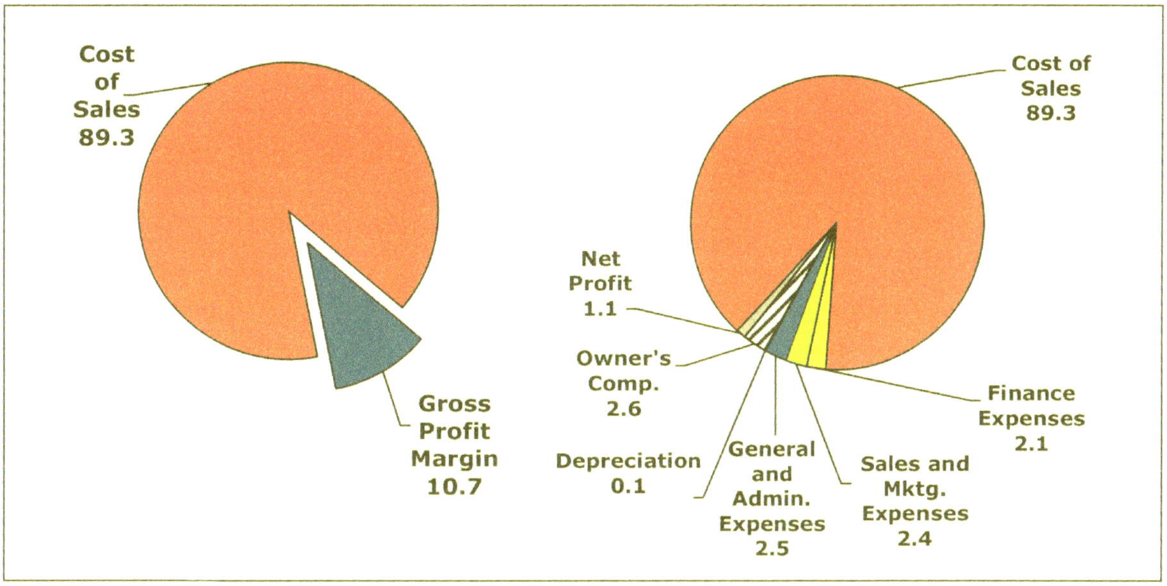

After a brief hiatus in 2017, when not enough data was collected to produce reliable results, this study brings back the average balance sheet for small builders with land costs. In 2020, this group of builders reported owning an average of $2.6 million in assets, 25% more than in 2014 ($2.1 million). During this six-year period, current assets jumped from accounting for 84.7% of total assets to almost the entirety of them (98.1%) (table 5.7).

A look at their liabilities shows that small builders with land costs have become more leveraged. In 2014, 65.3% of their assets were financed through debt ($1.4 million); by 2020, that share had risen to 70.0% ($1.8 million). Small builders with land costs also increased their average invested capital during this period ($720,000 to $780,000), yet equity financed a smaller portion of assets in 2020 (30.0%) than in 2014 (34.7%).

Table 5.7. Small-volume builders with land costs: balance sheet

	2014		2017		2020	
	Average (in $1,000s)	**Share of total**	**Average (in $1,000s)**	**Share of total**	**Average (in $1,000s)**	**Share of total**
Assets						
Current assets						
Cash	305	14.7			305	11.8
Receivables & inventories	n/a	n/a			5.1	5.1
Construction work in progress	1,220	58.8	N/A		1,676	64.5
Other current assets	232	11.2			433	16.7
Total current assets	1,756	84.7			2,547	98.1
Other assets	318	15.3			49	1.9
Total assets	**2,074**	**100.0**			**2,597**	**100.0**
Liabilities						
Current liabilities	149	7.2			383	14.7
Construction loans payable	769	37.1			1,250	48.2
Total current liabilities	917	44.2			1,633	62.9
Long-term liabilities	n/a	n/a			152	5.8
Other long-term liabilities	437	21.1			32	1.2
Total liabilities	**1,354**	**65.3**			**1,817**	**70.0**
Owner's equity	**720**	**34.7**			**780**	**30.0**
Total liabilities & owner's equity	**2,074**	**100.0**			**2,597**	**100.0**

A net profit margin approaching zero, along with increased assets and debt, hurt the overall financial health of small-volume builders who only build on their lots. The current ratio fell from 1.91 in 2014 to 1.48 in 2020, while the debt-to-equity ratio increased from 1.88 to 2.29. This group of builders also became less effective at transforming assets and equity into profits, as their ROA fell from 14.2% to 1.3% and the ROE from 41.0% to 4.4% (table 5.8). These levels are dangerously low and efforts to increase profitability and reduce the size of the assets of these businesses are warranted.

Table 5.8. Small-volume builders with land costs: financial ratios

	2014	2017	2020
Current ratio	1.91	N/A	1.48
Debt-to-equity ratio	1.88		2.29
Return on assets (%)	14.20		1.30
Return on equity (%)	41.00		4.40

Small-Volume Combination Builders

The final section of this chapter turns to the performance of combination small-volume builders, firms with 25 or fewer closings that build both on their land as well as on their customers' land. In the previous study covering fiscal year 2017, not enough of this type of builder provided income statements to allow for the tabulation of average revenue and profit margins. That, fortunately, was not the case in 2020, when they reported an average of $5.1 in total revenue, essentially the same as in 2014 ($5.2 million).

A quick comparison of cost structures during this period shows another remarkable similarity: cost of sales took up 83.4% of all revenue in 2020, essentially the same as the 83.9% in 2014. There was, however, some shifting within those costs, as single-family direct construction costs rose from 64.4% of revenue to 70.9%, while those related to remodeling, multifamily, and light commercial fell from 8.3% to 4.5%. Small combination builders averaged $854,000 in gross profits in 2020 — a gross margin of 16.6% that is essentially unchanged from 2014 (16.1%) (table 5.9).

Table 5.9. Small-volume combination builders: gross profit

	2014		2017		2020	
	Average ($1,000s)	**Share of revenue (%)**	**Average ($1,000s)**	**Share of revenue (%)**	**Average ($1,000s)**	**Share of revenue (%)**
Revenue	5,160	100.0			5,149	100.0
Cost of sales						
Land costs	384	7.4	N/A		268	5.2
Direct costs: single-family	3,322	64.4			3,649	70.9
Direct costs: multifamily, remodeling, light commercial/industrial	428	8.3			230	4.5
Indirect construction costs	137	2.7			147	2.9
Other costs	58	1.1			1	0.0
Total cost of sales	4,330	83.9			4,295	83.4
Gross profit	**830**	**16.1**			**854**	**16.6**

The share of revenue small combination builders spent on operating expenses has not changed significantly in the past six years. In 2020, 11.7% of their revenue was spent covering financing, sales & marketing, and general & administrative expenses, depreciation, and owner's compensation. In 2014, that share had been 11.1%. Given how little the overall structure of their income statements changed during this period, small combination builders reported about the same net profit margin in 2020 (4.9%) as they did in 2014 (5.0%) (table 5.10). Figure 5.3 summarizes the income statements for small-volume combination builders for 2020 (Appendix V.5.).

Table 5.10. Small-volume combination builders: net profit

	2014		2017		2020	
	Average ($1,000s)	Share of revenue (%)	Average ($1,000s)	Share of revenue (%)	Average ($1,000s)	Share of revenue (%)
Gross profit	830	16.1			854	16.6
Operating expenses						
Financing expenses	56	1.1	N/A		42	0.8
Sales & mktg. expenses	114	2.2			117	2.3
General & administrative expenses	283	5.5			278	5.4
Depreciation	n/a	n/a			17	0.3
Owner's compensation	120	2.3			149	2.9
Total operating expenses	573	11.1			603	11.7
Net profit (loss)	**257**	**5.0**			**251**	**4.9**

Figure 5.3. Small-volume combination builders: cost of sales, expenses, and net profit (% of revenue)

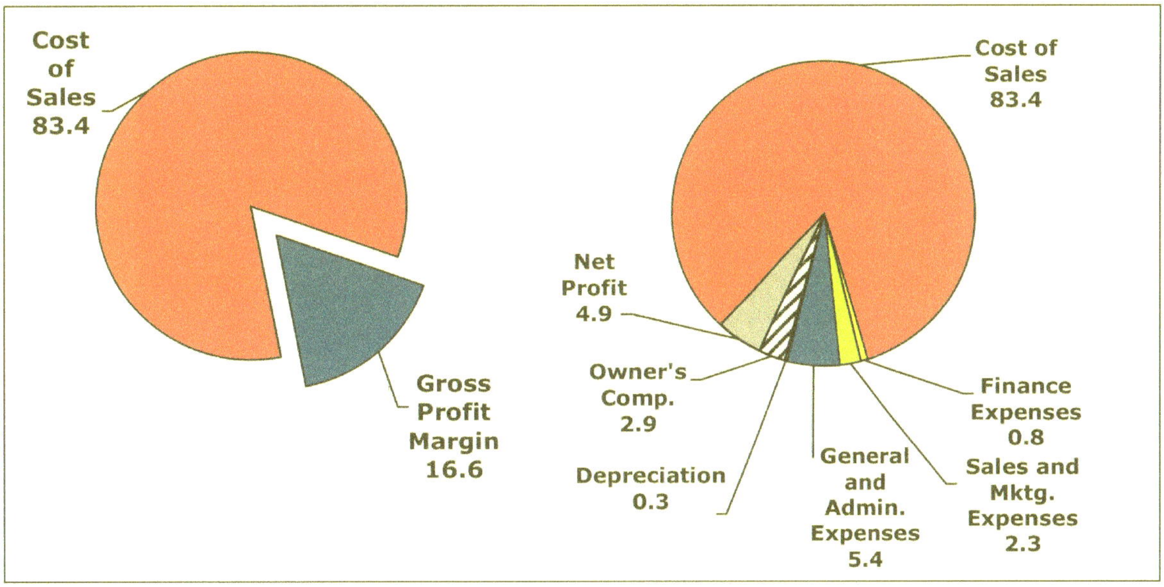

Total assets for small combination builders averaged $3.1 million in 2020, about 9% lower than in 2014 ($3.5 million). No comparisons will be made to 2017 because the data for that year seem anomalously low compared to the historical series for this group of builders. A highlight in 2020 is that 95.3% of all their assets were in the form of current assets, a significant jump from the 84.2% they represented in 2014.

Meanwhile, total liabilities for this subset of builders averaged $2.5 million in 2020, not much different from the $2.4 million they owed in 2014. What did change during this period was the average amount small combination builders held as equity in their companies: that went from $1.1 million in 2014 to only $669,000 in 2020. As a result, the share of assets financed through equity dropped from 30.5% to 21.3% (table 5.11).

Table 5.11. Small-volume combination builders: balance sheet

	2014		2017		2020	
	Average ($1,000s)	Share of total (%)	Average ($1,000s)	Share of total (%)	Average ($1,000s)	Share of total (%)
Assets						
Current assets						
Cash	362	10.5	264	23.6	458	14.6
Receivables and inventories	n/a	n/a	126	11.3	364	11.6
Construction work in progress	1,900	54.8	515	46.2	1,931	61.5
Other current assets	656	18.9	105	9.4	238	7.6
Total current assets	2,919	84.2	1,011	90.5	2,991	95.3
Other assets	546	15.8	106	9.5	148	4.7
Total assets	**3,465**	**100.0**	**1,116**	**100.0**	**3,139**	**100.0**
Liabilities						
Current liabilities	738	21.3	363	32.5	1,047	33.3
Construction loans payable	1,316	38.0	148	13.3	1,312	41.8
Total current liabilities	2,054	59.3	511	45.8	2,359	75.2
Long-term loans payable	n/a	n/a	22	2.0	49	1.5
Other long-term liabilities	356	10.3	7	0.6	63	2.0
Total liabilities	**2,410**	**69.5**	**540**	**48.4**	**2,470**	**78.7**
Owner's equity	**1,055**	**30.5**	**576**	**51.6**	**669**	**21.3**
Total liabilities & owner's equity	**3,465**	**100.0**	**1,116**	**100.0**	**3,139**	**100.0**

Financial ratios for small combination builders showed some deterioration in 2020. The current ratio was only 1.27 (down from 1.42 in 2014) and the debt-to-equity ratio shot up to 3.69 (from 2.28 in 2014). As a point of reference, a debt-to-equity ratio above 4.0 is considered so risky that most financial institutions would likely turn down additional borrowing requests from any company with that level of debt. Looked at another way, a D/E ratio of 4.0 says that 80% of the assets are funded by borrowed money and the owner's investment, i.e. risk, is only at 20%.

Similar rates of return and levels of assets in 2014 and 2020 led the group's ROA to remain essentially unchanged during this period, barely moving from 7.4% to 8.0%. Producing about the same net profit with lower amounts of capital did lead to an improvement in their ROE, which rose from 24.4% to 37.5% (table 5.12).

Table 5.12. Small-volume combination builders: financial ratios

	2014	2017	2020
Current ratio	1.42	1.98	1.27
Debt-to-equity ratio	2.28	0.94	3.69
Return on assets (%)	7.40	n/a	8.00
Return on equity (%)	24.40	n/a	37.50

6

Production Builders

All Production Builders Combined

For the purpose of this study, a production builder is one that closes 26 or more units per year. According to the 2020 NAHB Builder Member Census, approximately 17% of our association's single-family builder members fall under this classification. Total revenue for the typical production builder in 2020 was $29.6 million, about 1% lower than in 2017 ($29.8 million), and 5% below the level in 2014 ($31.1 million). On average, these builders spent 80.6% of revenue ($23.8 million) on costs of sales, down from 81.2% in 2017. Most of the reduction in costs came from direct construction costs for single-family homes, which as a share of revenue declined from 62.5% in 2017 to 60.0% in 2020. Production builders finished fiscal year 2020 with $5.7 million in gross profits, which translates into a 19.4% gross margin — the largest gross profit margin for this group of builders since 2006's 21.3% (table 6.1).

Table 6.1. Gross profit

	2014		2017		2020	
	Average ($1,000s)	Share of revenue (%)	Average ($1,000s)	Share of revenue (%)	Average ($1,000s)	Share of revenue (%)
Revenue	31,089	100.0	29,766	100.0	29,568	100.0
Cost of sales						
Land costs	4,847	15.6	3,870	13.0	4,388	14.8
Direct costs: single-family	18,627	59.9	18,613	62.5	17,751	60.0
Direct costs: multifamily, remodeling, light commercial/industrial	396	1.3	744	2.5	730	2.5
Indirect construction costs	894	2.9	836	2.8	950	3.2
Other costs	431	1.4	95	0.3	10	0.0
Total cost of sales	25,195	81.0	24,158	81.2	23,830	80.6
Gross profit	**5,894**	**19.0**	**5,608**	**18.8**	**5,738**	**19.4**

In addition to squeezing costs of sales to their lowest point in a decade and a half, production builders also continued to keep a lid on operating expenses. In 2020, they spent 11.8% of revenue on expenses, barely higher than in 2017 (11.4%). At their peak in 2008, production builders had spent a whopping 18.9% of revenue on these expenses, but then managed to drive them down over the following years. They finished fiscal year 2020 with an average $2.3 million in net profits, which translates into a 7.6% net profit margin. That was just a hair higher than in 2017 (7.5%) and the highest seen by this group of builders since 2006's 8.4% (table 6.2). Figure 6.1 summarizes the income statements for production builders in 2020 (Appendix V.3.).

Table 6.2. Net profit

	2014		2017		2020	
	Average ($1,000s)	**Share of revenue (%)**	**Average ($1,000s)**	**Share of revenue (%)**	**Average ($1,000s)**	**Share of revenue (%)**
Gross profit	5,894	19.0	5,608	18.8	5,738	19.4
Operating expenses						
Financing expenses	518	1.7	398	1.3	457	1.5
Sales & mktg. expenses	1,667	5.4	1,479	5.0	1,473	5.0
General & administrative expenses	1,242	4.0	1,220	4.1	1,301	4.4
Depreciation	n/a	n/a	35	0.1	30	0.1
Owner's compensation	360	1.2	254	0.9	219	0.7
Total operating expenses	3,788	12.2	3,386	11.4	3,481	11.8
Net profit (loss)	**2,106**	**6.8**	**2,221**	**7.5**	**2,257**	**7.6**

Figure 6.1. Cost of sales, expenses, and net profit (% of revenue)

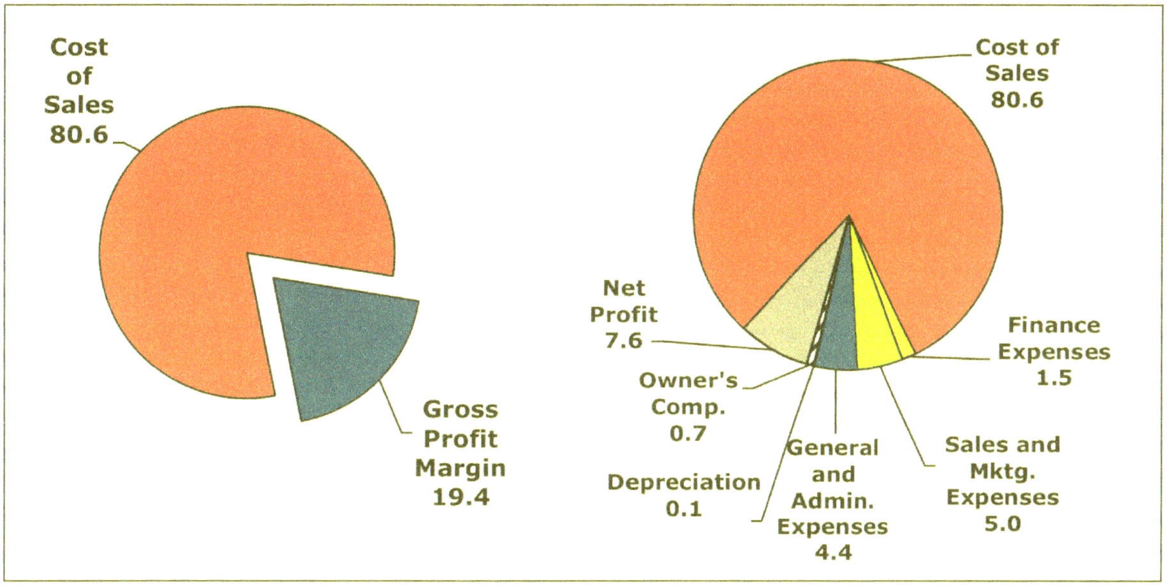

Production builders expanded their balance sheets between 2017 and 2020, as their average total assets grew 17% from $14.5 million to $16.9 million. There were two significant shifts in the composition of assets during this period. One, construction work in progress dropped from representing 72.2% of all assets in 2017 to 63.5% in 2020. And two, cash rose in prominence, doubling its share of assets from 6.4% to 13.3%. In contrast to small builders, for whom current assets became significantly more relevant during this period, their share fell from 92.0% to 89.9% among production builders (table 6.3).

The recent increase in assets was financed mostly by increased equity instead of debt. From 2017 to 2020, this group's average liabilities only grew by 6%, from $10.3 million to $10.9 million. Equity, on the other hand, rose by 46%, from $4.1 million to $6.1 million. As a result, the share of assets financed through the owner's invested capital rose from 28.7% to 35.8%.

Table 6.3. Balance sheet

	2014		2017		2020	
	Average ($1,000s)	Share of total (%)	Average ($1,000s)	Share of total (%)	Average ($1,000s)	Share of total (%)
Assets						
Current assets						
Cash	1,178	5.9	924	6.4	2,250	13.3
Receivables and inventories	n/a	n/a	905	6.3	1,439	8.5
Construction work in progress	14,378	72.4	10,440	72.2	10,769	63.5
Other current assets	2,604	13.1	1,034	7.2	774	4.6
Total current assets	18,160	91.5	13,302	92.0	15,233	89.9
Other assets	1,690	8.5	1,151	8.0	1,713	10.1
Total assets	**19,850**	**100.0**	**14,454**	**100.0**	**16,946**	**100.0**
Liabilities						
Current liabilities	3,836	19.3	3,819	26.4	5,271	31.1
Construction loans payable	7,322	36.9	5,141	35.6	3,582	21.1
Total current liabilities	11,157	56.2	8,960	62.0	8,853	52.2
Long-term loans payable	n/a	n/a	1,305	9.0	1,777	10.5
Other long-term liabilities	2,433	12.3	43	0.3	255	1.5
Total liabilities	**13,590**	**68.5**	**10,308**	**71.3**	**10,885**	**64.2**
Owner's equity	**6,260**	**31.5**	**4,146**	**28.7**	**6,061**	**35.8**
Total liabilities & owner's equity	**19,850**	**100.0**	**14,454**	**100.0**	**16,946**	**100.0**

The ratios analyzed in this study show production builders are financially healthy companies. From 2017 to 2020, the current ratio rose from 1.48 to 1.72, thus demonstrating increased liquidity in their operations. The debt-to-equity ratio dropped from 2.49 to 1.80, which showcases the group's decreased reliance on debt to run their businesses. More assets and equity, but about the same level of net returns, caused the ROA and ROE to lose some ground in 2020, to still healthy levels of 13.3% and 37.2%, respectively (table 6.4).

Table 6.4. Financial ratios

	2014	2017	2020
Current ratio	1.63	1.48	1.72
Debt-to-equity ratio	2.17	2.49	1.80
Return on assets (%)	10.60	15.40	13.30
Return on equity (%)	33.60	53.60	37.20

Production Builders with Land Costs

Much like the previous chapter analyzed results for different types of small-volume builders, the rest of this chapter breaks down production builders into two different subsets. This first section analyzes the performance of production builders with land costs, in other words, builders with 26 or more closings a year who only build spec or pre-sold homes on their own lots. The following section will analyze the performance of combination production builders, who also have 26 or more closings, but build both on their land as well as on their customers' land.

In the previous study covering fiscal year 2017, not enough production builders with land costs provided income statements to allow for the tabulation of average revenue and profit margins. That, fortunately, was not the case in 2020, when their total revenue averaged \$31.2 million, up 6% from 2014 (\$33.2 million) (table 6.5). Altogether, cost of sales took up 79.4% of revenue in 2020, which left them with a gross profit margin of 20.6% (\$6.4 million) — the highest gross margin reported by this subset of builders since 2006's 22.1%.

Table 6.5. Production builders with land costs: gross profit

	2014		2017		2020	
	Average (\$1,000s)	Share of revenue (%)	Average (\$1,000s)	Share of revenue (%)	Average (\$1,000s)	Share of revenue (%)
Revenue	33,192	100.0			31,209	100.0
Cost of sales						
Land costs	5,317	16.0	N/A		5,418	17.4
Direct costs: single-family	19,848	59.8			18,186	58.3
Direct costs: multifamily, remodeling, light commercial/industrial	417	1.3			0	0
Indirect construction costs	852	2.6			1,167	3.7
Other costs	795	2.4			10	0.0
Total cost of sales	27,230	82.0			24,781	79.4
Gross profit	**5,962**	**18.0**			**6,428**	**20.6**

Meanwhile, production builders with land costs saw operating expenses take up a slightly larger share of revenue in 2020 (13.1%) than in 2014 (12.3%) (table 6.6). The expense line with the most growth was general & administrative expenses, which went from taking up 4.1% of revenue to 5.1%. The largest change was in owner's compensation, which fell from $431,000 to $165,000 and from 1.3% to 0.5% of revenue. In the end, this group of builders posted a net profit margin of 7.5% ($2.3 million), the highest point for this series since 2006's 9.3%. Figure 6.2 summarizes the 2020 income statement for production builders with land costs (Appendix V.4.).

Table 6.6. Production builders with land costs: net profit

	2014		2017		2020	
	Average ($1,000s)	Share of revenue (%)	Average ($1,000s)	Share of revenue (%)	Average ($1,000s)	Share of revenue (%)
Gross profit	5,962	18.0			6,428	20.6
Operating expenses						
Financing expenses	639	1.9	N/A		541	1.7
Sales & mktg. expenses	1,644	5.0			1,771	5.7
General & administrative expenses	1,358	4.1			1,600	5.1
Depreciation	n/a	n/a			10	0.0
Owner's compensation	431	1.3			165	0.5
Total operating expenses	4,073	12.3			4,087	13.1
Net profit (loss)	**1,890**	**5.7**			**2,340**	**7.5**

Figure 6.2. Production builders with land costs: cost of sales, expenses, and net profit (% of revenue)

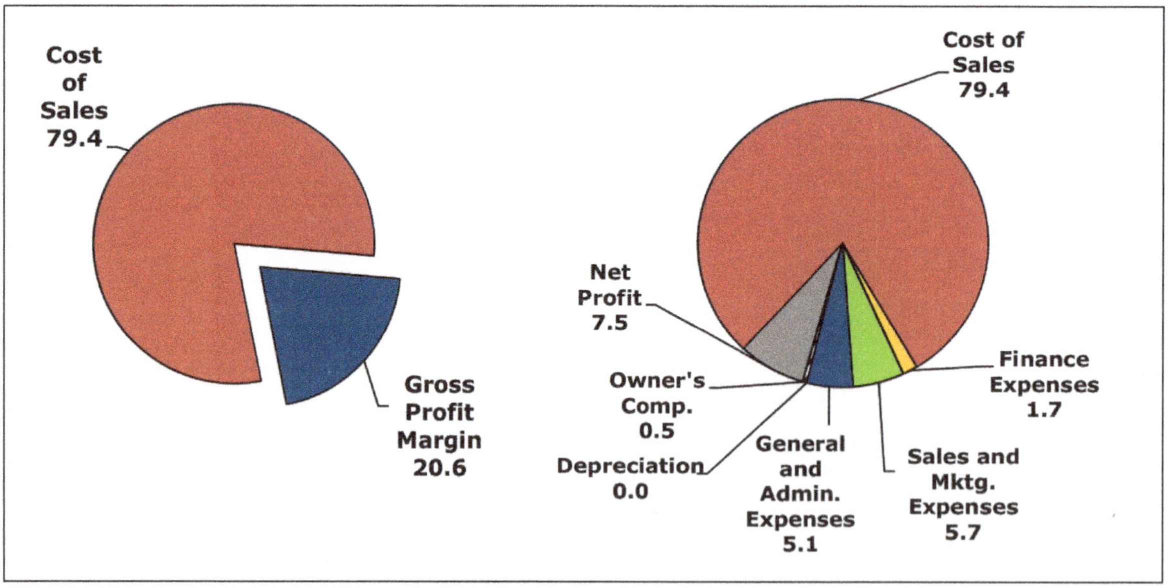

This year's edition also brings back the average balance sheet for production builders with land costs, after sample size issues suppressed it in 2017. In 2020, this group of builders averaged $17.6 million in total assets, nearly 25% fewer assets than in 2014 ($23.2 million) and the lowest point in this series since its inception in 2002. Cash was the only asset class to see an increase from 2014 to 2020 ($1.5 million to $2.2 million), in stark contrast to the drop experienced by all other types of assets. In fact, the share of assets held in cash nearly doubled, from 6.4% to 12.7% (table 6.7).

Further analysis of 2020 balance sheets for production builders with land costs reveals an interesting fact: these builders have undergone significant deleveraging. Between 2014 and 2020, their total liabilities went from averaging $17.6 million to $12.1 million — a noteworthy 31% decline in total debt. The owners' own invested capital, however, remained rather stable during this period, barely moving from $5.6 million to $5.5 million. The result of this dynamic was that equity ended up playing a larger role financing this group's operations, as the share of assets it supported rose from 24.2% to 31.2% (table 6.7).

Table 6.7. Production builders with land costs: balance sheet

	2014		2017		2020	
	Average ($1,000s)	Share of total (%)	Average ($1,000s)	Share of total (%)	Average ($1,000s)	Share of total (%)
Assets						
Current assets						
Cash	1,496	6.4	N/A		2,239	12.7
Receivables and inventories	n/a	n/a			828	4.7
Construction work in progress	15,683	67.6			12,331	70.0
Other current assets	3,462	14.9			477	2.7
Total current assets	20,641	89.0			15,874	90.1
Other assets	2,554	11.0			1,742	9.9
Total assets	**23,195**	**100.0**			**17,616**	**100.0**
Liabilities						
Current liabilities	5,056	21.8			6,075	34.5
Construction loans payable	8,544	36.8			3,642	20.7
Total current liabilities	13,600	58.6			9,717	55.2
Long-term loans payable	n/a	n/a			2,262	12.8
Other long-term loan liabilities	3,984	17.2			136	0.8
Total liabilities	**17,584**	**75.8**			**12,116**	**68.8**
Owner's equity	**5,610**	**24.2**			**5,500**	**31.2**
Total liabilities & owner's equity	**23,195**	**100.0**			**17,616**	**100.0**

Better returns produced with fewer assets meant healthier financial ratios for production builders with land costs. The ROA, for example, rose from 8.1% in 2014 to 13.3% in 2020, while the ROE improved from 33.7% to 42.6%. Lower levels of debt drove their debt-to-equity ratio down, from 3.13 to 2.18, while the current ratio remained essentially the same (1.52 to 1.55) (table 6.8).

Table 6.8. Production builders with land costs: financial ratios

	2014	2017	2020
Current ratio	1.52	N/A	1.55
Debt-to-equity ratio	3.13		2.18
Return on assets (%)	8.10		13.30
Return on equity (%)	33.70		42.60

Note: No data for production builders without land costs were produced because of insufficient sample size.

Production Combination Builders

The final section of this chapter turns to the performance of combination production builders, who are firms with 26 or more closings that build both on their land as well as on their customers' land. In the previous study covering fiscal year 2017, not enough of this type of builder provided income statements to allow for the tabulation of average revenue and profit margins. That was not the case in 2020. On average, this subset of builders earned $27.8 million in revenue that year, about 16% lower than in 2014 ($33.3 million) and the lowest average since 2010 ($18.4 million). Cost of sales in 2020 accounted for 82.0% of all revenue (up from 79.6% in 2014), leaving them with a gross profit margin of 18.0% ($5.0 million) — a decline from 2014's 20.4% gross margin (table 6.9).

Table 6.9. Production combination builders: gross profit

	2014		2017		2020	
	Average ($1,000s)	Share of revenue (%)	Average ($1,000s)	Share of revenue (%)	Average ($1,000s)	Share of revenue (%)
Revenue	33,251	100.0			27,790	100.0
Cost of sales						
Land costs	5,190	15.6	N/A		3,272	11.8
Direct costs: single-family	19,764	59.4			17,280	62.2
Direct costs: multifamily, remodeling, light commercial/industrial	415	1.2			1,522	5.5
Indirect construction costs	1,054	3.2			715	2.6
Other costs	32	0.1			11	0.0
Total cost of sales	26,454	79.6			22,799	82.0
Gross profit	**6,797**	**20.4**			**4,991**	**18.0**

Perhaps in response to that loss in gross margin, production combination builders squeezed a lot of fat out of operating expenses in 2020, spending only 10.2% of revenue on these expenses. That was two points lower than the 12.1% they spent in 2014 (table 6.10). In the end, the belt-tightening was not enough to overcome the drop in gross margin, so they finished fiscal year 2020 with a net profit margin of 7.8% ($2.2 million), down from 8.3% in 2014. Nonetheless, that 7.8% net margin was the second highest in this group's history — only behind 2014's 8.3%. Figure 6.3 summarizes the income statement for production combination builders for 2020 (Appendix V.5.).

Table 6.10. Production combination builders: net profit

	2014		2017		2020	
	Average ($1,000s)	Share of revenue (%)	Average ($1,000s)	Share of revenue (%)	Average ($1,000s)	Share of revenue (%)
Gross profit	6,797	20.4			4,991	18.0
Operating expenses						
Financing expenses	460	1.4	N/A		367	1.3
Sales & mktg. expenses	2,006	6.0			1,150	4.1
General & administrative expenses	1,270	3.8			977	3.5
Depreciation	n/a	n/a			52	0.2
Owner's compensation	295	0.9			278	1.0
Total operating expenses	4,031	12.1			2,824	10.2
Net profit (loss)	**2,766**	**8.3**			**2,167**	**7.8**

Figure 6.3. Production combination builders: cost of sales, expenses, and net profit (% of revenue)

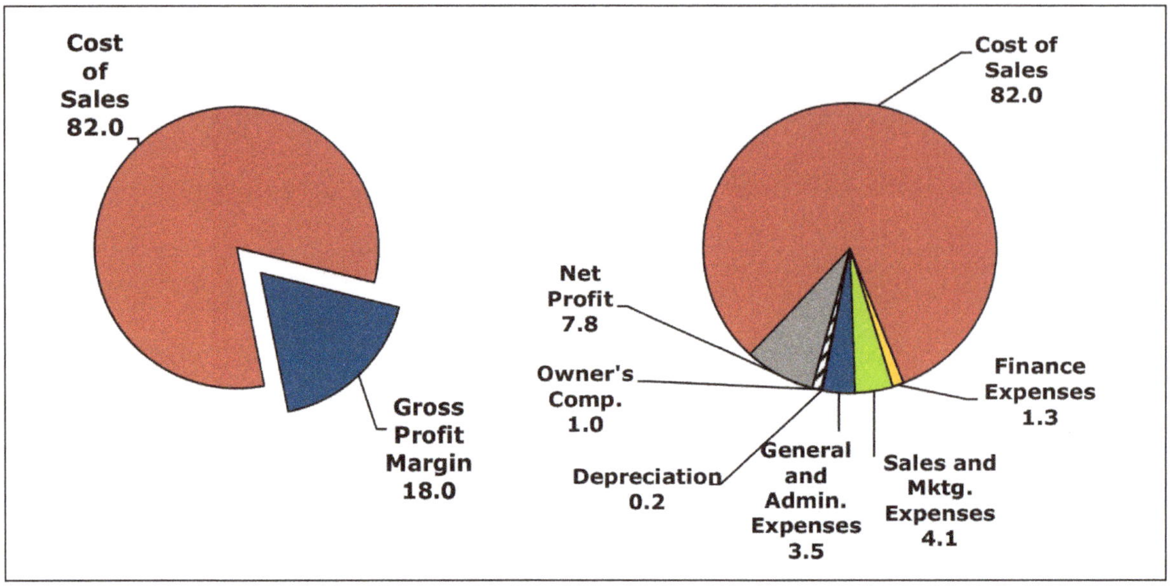

The total amount of assets owned by the average production combination builder did not change much between 2017 and 2020, but how those assets were paid for did shift significantly. This group of builders owned an average of $16.3 million in total assets in 2020, only about 2% fewer assets than in 2017 ($16.7 million) (but the lowest point in this series since 2010's $11.1 million). While the share of assets held in cash more than tripled from 2017 to 2020 (4.2% to 13.9%), the share held as construction work in progress sank from 75.6% to 56.6%. Altogether, current assets made up 89.7% of assets in 2020, down from 93.0% in 2017 (table 6.11).

The other side of the ledger shows the shift in how assets were paid for. Between 2017 and 2020, the total amount production combination builders owed to others declined from an average of $12.1 million to $9.7 million – a 20% reduction in debt. On the other side of the coin, their average invested capital jumped 44% during this period, from $4.6 million to $6.6 million. This translates into 40.7% of assets being financed via equity in 2020, up from 27.6% in 2017.

Table 6.11. Production combination builders: balance sheet

	2014		2017		2020	
	Average ($1,000s)	Share of total (%)	Average ($1,000s)	Share of total (%)	Average ($1,000s)	Share of total (%)
Assets						
Current assets						
Cash	944	5.1	694	4.2	2,261	13.9
Receivables and inventories	n/a	n/a	1,086	6.5	2,051	12.6
Construction work in progress	14,702	79.7	12,618	75.6	9,207	56.6
Other current assets	1,919	10.4	1,122	6.7	1,072	6.6
Total current assets	17,566	95.3	15,521	93.0	14,591	89.7
Other assets	876	4.7	1,160	7.0	1,684	10.3
Total assets	**18,442**	**100.0**	**16,681**	**100.0**	**16,275**	**100.0**
Liabilities						
Current liabilities	2,868	15.5	6,006	36.0	4,467	27.4
Construction loans payable	6,832	37.0	4,907	29.4	3,522	21.6
Total current liabilities	9,699	52.6	10,913	65.4	7,989	49.1
Long-term loans payable	n/a	n/a	1,081	6.5	1,292	7.9
Other long-term liabilities	896	4.9	77	0.5	374	2.3
Total liabilities	**10,595**	**57.5**	**12,070**	**72.4**	**9,654**	**59.3**
Owner's equity	**7,847**	**42.5**	**4,610**	**27.6**	**6,621**	**40.7**
Total liabilities & owner's equity	**18,442**	**100.0**	**16,681**	**100.0**	**16,275**	**100.0**

The financial health of production combination builders is strong. A large drop in current liabilities led to an increase in their current ratio from 1.42 in 2017 to 1.83 in 2020, while the drastic overall decline in liabilities drove the debt-to-equity ratio down from 2.62 to 1.46. The ROA and ROE measures did not change much since the last time they were calculated in 2014 and remain at healthy levels (ROA=13.3% and ROE=32.7%) (table 6.12).

Table 6.12. Production combination builders: financial ratios

	2014	2017	2020
Current ratio	1.81	1.42	1.83
Debt-to-equity ratio	1.35	2.62	1.46
Return on assets (%)	15.00	n/a	13.30
Return on equity (%)	35.20	n/a	32.70

7

Builder Financial Performance by Region and Business Model

Single-family home building was by far the primary source of revenue for builders responding to this edition of *The Cost of Doing Business Study,* originating 93.8% of the average $13.7 million they earned in 2020. Residential remodeling accounted for only 2.5% of that revenue, followed by 1.1% from light commercial/industrial building, 0.8% from multifamily building, and 1.8% from all other sources combined.

Revenue and Profits by Region

Builders in every region of the U.S. reported earning over 90% of their 2020 revenue from single-family home building. In the West, at the most extreme, 98.4% of revenue came from that single source. The share was 92.7% in the South and 91.0% in the Midwest. A breakdown of the income statement cannot be produced for the Northeast because insufficient responses from this region make any estimates statistically unreliable.

Builders in the South spent 12.0% of their revenue in 2020 on land costs, slightly lower than what builders in the Midwest spent (12.6%) and well below what land cost builders in the West (14.0%). Builders in the West also reported spending 63.3% of all their revenue on direct construction costs for single-family home building (i.e. labor and materials) – the most of any region. In the South that share was 59.0% and in the Midwest 60.0%. After accounting for these and other costs of sales, however, builders in the West finished 2020 with the highest gross profit margin of any region, at 19.7%, followed by the South (17.7%) and not far behind that by the Midwest (17.6%) (fig. 7.1).

On average, builders in the South spent the smallest proportion of revenue on operating expenses, at 10.6%. Those in the West and Midwest spent about one percentage point more, at 11.6% and 11.7%, respectively. The most important of these expenses in the

Midwest and South was general and administrative expenses, which accounted for 4.9% and 4.2% of revenue, respectively. In the West, the largest share paid for sales and marketing expenses, was 4.7%. After subtracting all expenses from gross profits, builders in the West reported the highest net profit margin of all three regions, at 8.0%, compared with 7.1% in the South and 5.9% in the Midwest.

Quite impressively, Southern builders have been able to consistently improve their bottom line in every iteration of this study in the last decade. In 2010, they reported an average net profit margin of only 1.7%. By 2012, it was 3.5%; by 2014, 6.1%; by 2017, 6.4%; and by 2020, 7.1%. Builders in the West saw increases from 2010 (-2.9%) to 2017 (11.0%), before their net margin fell in 2020 (8.0). Meanwhile, the net margin improved for builders in the Midwest from 2010 (0.9%) to 2014 (7.3%), but has now fallen consecutively in 2017 (6.7%) and 2020 (5.9%).

Figure 7.1. Regional differences in costs and profit margins (% of revenue)

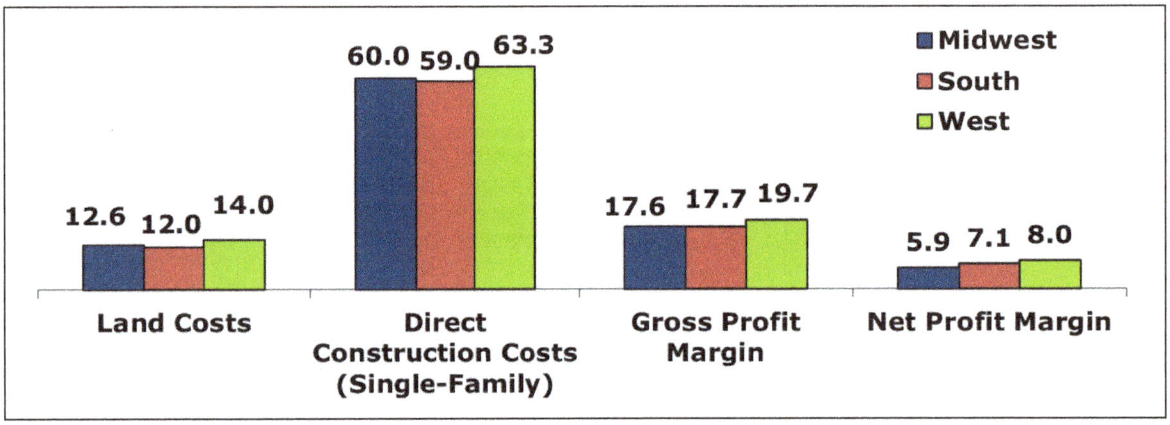

Revenue and Profits by Business Model

Historical data for the past five *Cost of Doing Business Studies,* spanning from 2010 to 2020, show that no single business model has won the 'most profitable' title on a consistent basis. Builders with land costs, for example, were the most profitable of the three models in 2012 (with a net margin of 6.2%) and 2017 (10.3%), but the title went to combination builders in 2014 (7.6%) and 2020 (7.2%). Builders without land costs were the most profitable model only once during this period, in 2010 (2.9%).

Figure 7.2 provides further profitability details for each of the three business models for fiscal year 2020. Combination builders averaged $15.2 million in total revenue, of which 82.3% went to pay for cost of sales, leaving them with a gross profit margin of 17.7%. Their owners received compensation equivalent to 1.4% of revenue. In the end, this group of builders had the highest net profit margin of the three business models, at 7.2%.

For their part, builders with land costs reported an average of $14.2 million in 2020, then went on to spend 80.7% of it on cost of sales, which left them with a gross margin of 19.3%. They only paid their owners 0.8% of revenue in compensation. After accounting for all costs and expenses, this group reported the second highest net profit margin of the three business models, at 6.6%.

Lastly, $8.7 million was the average revenue earned by builders without land costs in 2020. A hefty 86.8% of that amount was used to pay for costs of sales, which means their gross margin was only 13.2%. Owners at these companies received 3.5% of total revenue as compensation. That and other expenses left them with the lowest net profit margin of the three models, at 4.5%.

Although comparing net profit margins across business models is useful, it may not tell the complete story on profitability. A more comprehensive way to look at a builder's overall performance is to add the company's net profit margin to the share spent on owner's compensation, because there may be little distinction between the two items, especially, in small companies. According to this broader measure of profitability for 2020, combination builders were the best performers (8.6%), followed by builders without land costs (8.0%), and then those with land costs (7.4%). It should not escape the reader how counterintuitive it is for builders with land costs to be last in this overall measure of performance, despite posting the largest gross profit margin of the three business models.

Figure 7.2. Profits and owner's compensation by business model (% of revenue)

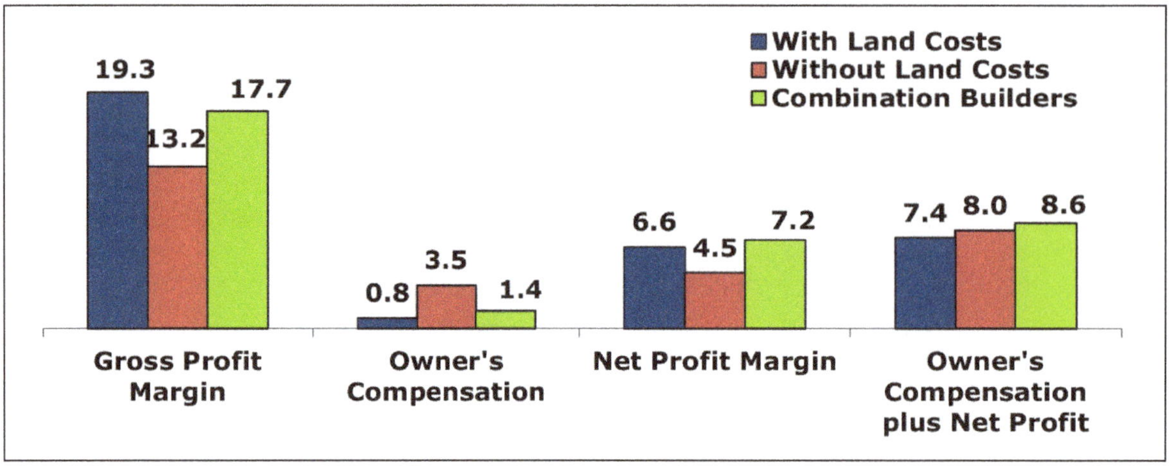

Builders with land costs had the largest balance sheets, with an average $9.5 million in total assets. Of that amount, $6.5 million was held as construction work in progress (69%) and $1.2 million as cash (13%). Current and long-term liabilities averaged $6.5 million (69% of assets), while owner's equity averaged $2.9 million (31% of assets) (fig. 7.3).

Combination builders followed closely with an average $9.3 million in total assets. They held $5.4 million of that as construction work in progress (57%) and another $1.3 million in cash (14%). This group of builders owed a total of $5.9 million (63% of assets) and had equity in their companies worth $3.5 million (37% of all assets).

Of the three business models, builders without land costs had the lowest average assets at $5.4 million. About $4.3 million of that was held as construction work in progress (81%), but only $294,000 was in cash (5%). This group of builders reported an average of $1.5 million (28% of assets) in total liabilities and $3.9 million in equity (72% of assets) (Appendix V).

Figure 7.3. Balance sheet by business model ($ averages in millions)

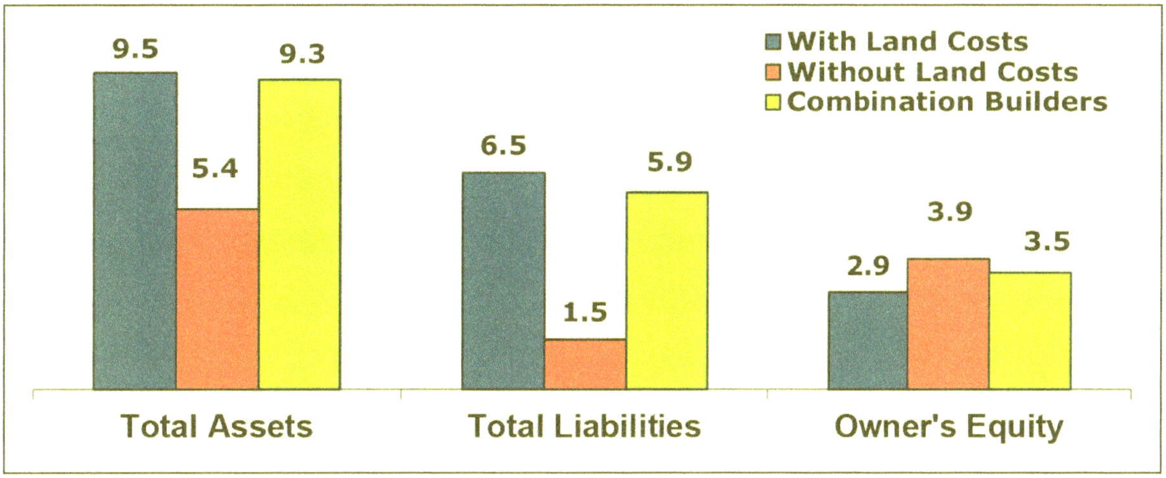

8

Operations

The vast majority — 90% — of respondents to this edition of *The Cost of Doing Business Study* are primarily single-family home builders. More specifically, 39% reported to be single-family custom builders on owners' lots, 26% were single-family production builders, and 25% single-family custom builders on the builder's lots (fig 8.1). Another 6% of respondents were primarily residential remodelers, 2% were multifamily builders, and 1% land developers. As stated previously, only respondents whose primary operation was single-family home building were included in the financial analysis presented throughout this report.

Figure 8.1. Main operation (% of respondents)

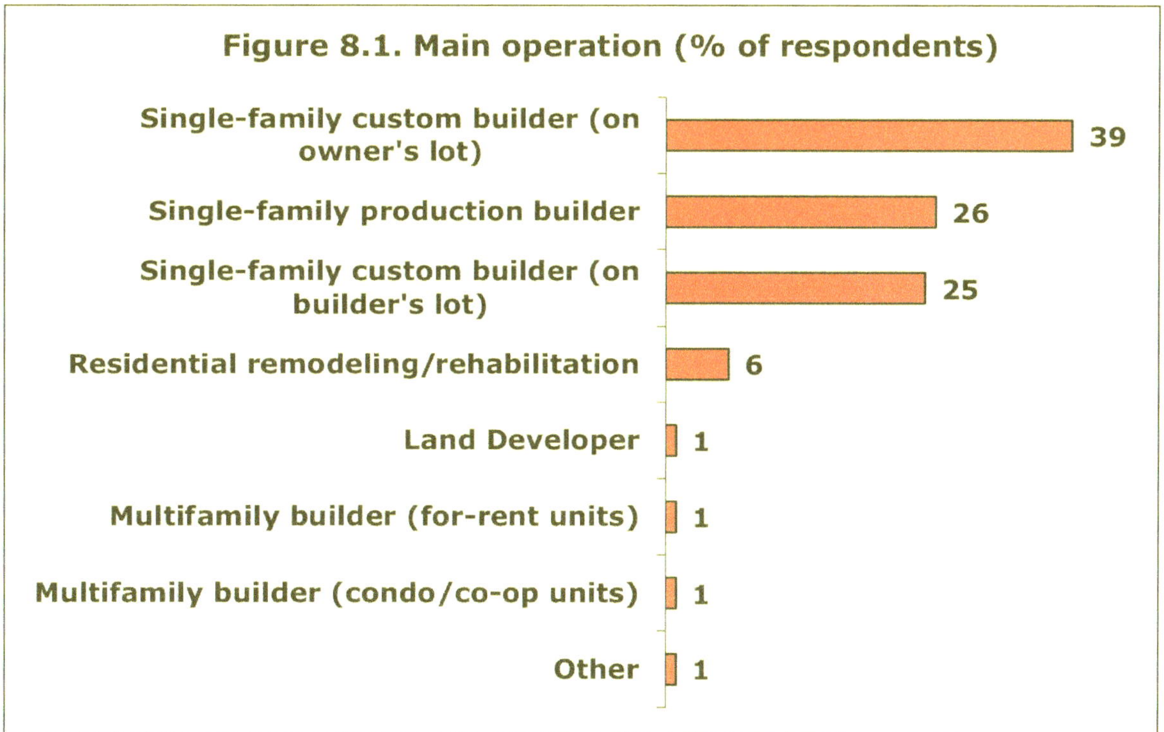

Number of Years in Business

Respondents to the latest *The Cost of Doing Business Study* have been in business for an average of 25 years. Only 18% have been in the residential construction industry for 10 years or less, 21% for 11 to 19 years, 22% for 20 to 29 years, and the remaining 39% for 30 years or longer (fig. 8.2).

Results show a direct positive relationship between years in business and the amount of revenue builders earned in 2020. Among those with less than $2 million in revenue, for example, average tenure in the industry was 17 years, compared to an average of 25 years among those earning $2 million to $9.9 million, and 27 years among those with revenue of $10 million or more (Appendix V.1.).

Looking at tenure across business models shows that builders with land costs have been in business slightly longer (25 years on average) than builders without land costs or combination builders (both 24 years). Across regions of the country, builders in the Northeast have been in business the longest, at an average of 32 years. Builders in the Midwest average 30 years in business, those in the South 24 years, and those in the West 23 years.

Figure 8.2. Years in the residential construction business (% of respondents)

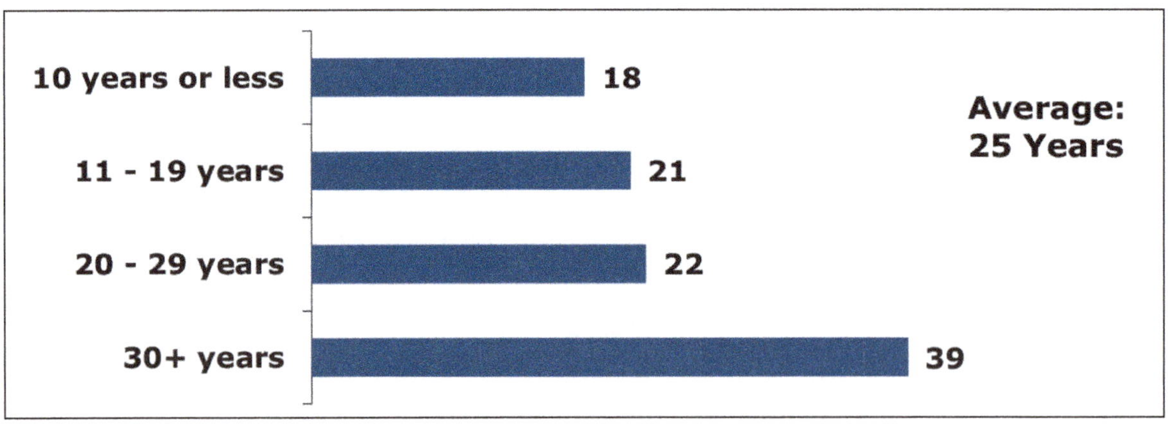

Units Closed: Presold, Speculative, or on Customers' Land

Respondents to *The Cost of Doing Business Study* closed an average of 26 units in 2020. Of those, 14 (54%) were pre-sold on the builders' lots, severn (27%) were built speculatively (without a buyer at the time of start), and five (19%) were built directly on the owner's land (fig 8.3). Builders' average number of closings in 2020 was higher than in 2008 and 2010 (24 units both years), but lower than in 2012 (46 units), 2014 (42 units), or 2017 (38 units). Data from the U.S. Census Bureau on the purpose of construction show that 78% of all single-family units started in 2020 were built for sale (either pre-sold or spec), 12% were built on the owner's land by a contractor, and 5% were built directly by the owner. The remaining 4% were built for-rent.

Builders with land costs closed an average of 36 single-family homes in 2020 (23 pre-sold, 13 speculative), just three fewer homes than in 2017 (39). Given the 17% increase in overall single-family production nationwide between 2017 and 2020 (from 849,000 to 991,000 units started), this decline is likely the result of a shift in the mix of builders responding to the survey in 2020 rather than an actual decline in the levels of production among builders with land costs during this period.

Builders without land costs closed an average of seven homes on land owned by their customers, a significant decline from the 21 homes this type of builder reported closing in 2017. Given the history for this group of builders, the 21 closings in 2017 were likely an anomaly in this series.

Combination builders, meanwhile, closed on 26 single-family homes in 2020, far fewer than the 45 closings this group reported in 2017. Of the 26 closings, 14 were pre-sold, six speculative, and seven were built on the owner's land (rounding of averages may cause the sum not to add up to the total number of closings).

Figure 8.3. Average number of homes closed in 2020 by type of builder

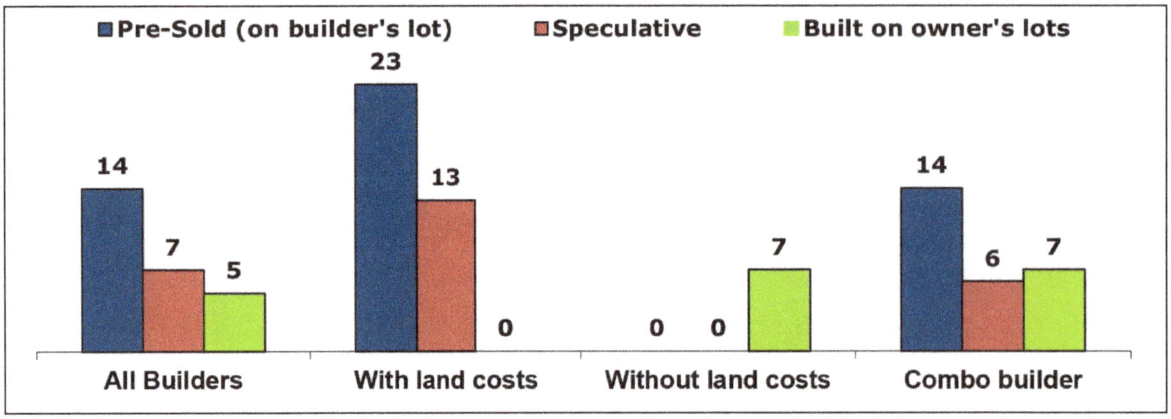

9

Historical Data and Trends

Analysis of historical data from *The Cost of Doing Business Study* reveals that in the 20-year span between 2000 and 2020, single-family builders averaged a net profit margin of 5.1%. In 2008, builders reported the worst financial performance in the history of the series, with a net profit margin of -3.0%. In 2010, they barely broke even (0.5%). But by 2012, they had returned to healthier net profits (4.9%), and the improvement continued into 2014 (6.4%) and 2017 (7.6%). In 2020 however, the rising trend ended, as their net margin declined slightly to 7.0% (fig. 9.1).

Figure 9.1. Builders' net profit margins since 2000 (% of revenue)

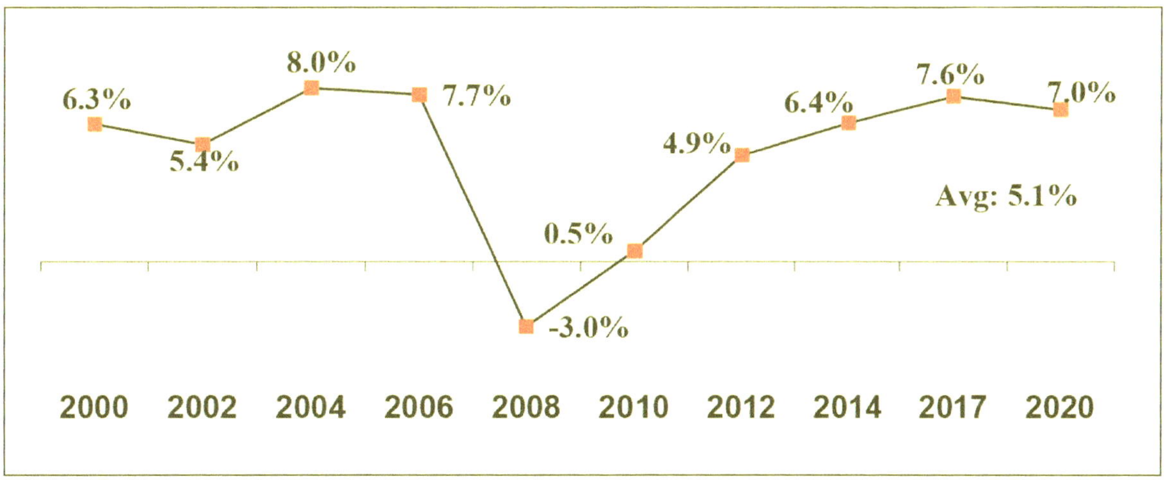

Costs of sales (land, direct, and indirect construction costs) as a share of total revenue peaked in 2008 at 85.6%, but then went on to decline steadily in every iteration of the study through 2017, when it reached 81.0%. In 2020, however, that trend also ended, as cost of sales rose to take up 81.8% of all revenue builders earned that year (table 9.1).

The average gross profit margin for builders responding to *The Cost of Doing Business Study* between 2000 and 2020 was 18.4%. Not surprisingly, the lowest gross margin happened during the Great Recession in 2008 (14.4%), but as explained in the paragraph above, builders countered the heavy losses that year by curtailing their cost of sales during the following years. That led to their gross profit margin improving steadily, first to 15.3% in 2010, and then to 17.4% in 2012, 18.9% in 2014, and 19.0% in 2017. The gains in their average gross margin ended in 2020, when it slid down to 18.2% (fig. 9.2).

Figure 9.2. Builders' gross profit margins since 2000 (% of revenue)

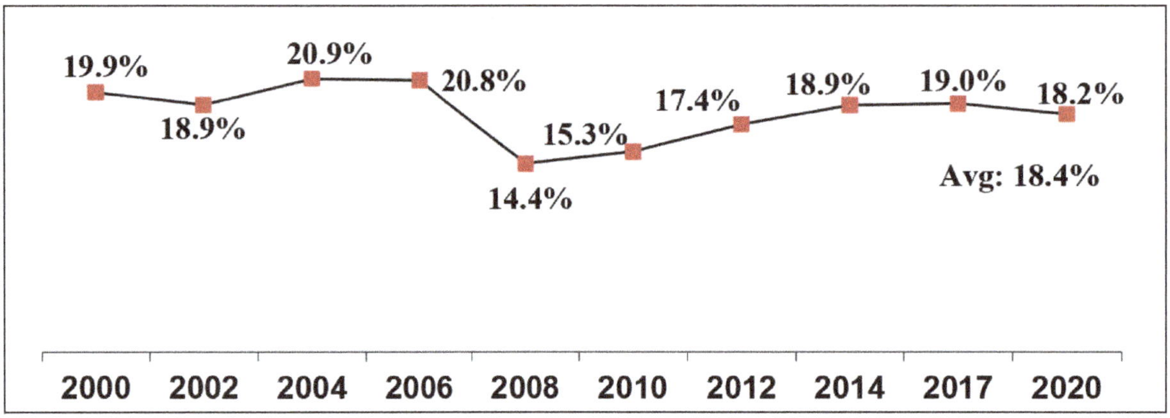

Operating expenses as a share of revenue rose significantly during the housing recession, but have eased since then. In 2006, they accounted for 13.1% of all revenue, before jumping to 17.4% in 2008. In the years since, builders have been extremely successful at squeezing the fat out of these expenses. In 2010, they took up 14.7% of revenue, but by 2020, the share was only 11.2% (table 9.1).

Table 9.1. Summary data from the NAHB *Cost of Doing Business Studies* (% of revenue)

	Total Sales	Cost of Sales	Gross Profit	Operating Expenses Breakdown					Total Operating Expense	Net Income Before Tax
				Finance	Sales and Marketing	General & Administrative	Depreciation	Owner's Compensation		
2020	100	81.8	18.2	1.3	4.1	4.4	0.1	1.3	11.2	7.0
2017	100	81.0	19.0	1.3	4.7	4.1	0.1	1.2	11.4	7.6
2014	100	81.1	18.9	1.4	5.0	4.7		1.3	12.5	6.4
2012	100	82.6	17.4	1.7	5.1	5.0		0.8	12.5	4.9
2010	100	84.7	15.3	2.1	5.2	5.8		1.6	14.7	0.5
2008	100	85.6	14.4	2.8	5.4	7.5		1.7	17.4	-3.0
2006	100	79.2	20.8	2.5	4.4	5.0		1.3	13.1	7.7
2004	100	79.1	20.9	1.5	4.7	5.4		1.3	12.9	8.0
2002	100	81.1	18.9	0.6	2.6	5.9		4.5	13.6	5.4
2000	100	80.1	19.9	2.2	5.7	3.9		1.8	13.5	6.3
1996	100	82.4	17.6	1.5	3.3	5.0		3.4	13.2	4.4
1993	100	79.4	20.6	1.9	4.0	5.1		5.0	16.0	4.6
1991	100	78.0	22.0	3.0	4.0	5.0			12.0	10.0
1989	100	79.1	20.9	5.6	5.2	4.8			15.6	5.3
1987	100	79.7	20.3	3.3	3.7	6.1			13.1	7.2
1985	100	81.7	18.3	3.9	3.3	7.6			14.8	3.5
1983*	100	79.7	20.3	4.5	3.3	8.8			17.6	2.7
1980*	100	77.2	22.8	2.0	2.5	9.4			16.9	5.9
1978	100	76.1	23.9	2.7	3.6	5.5			16.9	7.0
1975	100	84.1	15.9	2.8	2.3	7.5			11.6	4.3
1970	100	82.4	17.6	3.3	3.0	6.5			14.4	3.2

* The Values for 1980 and 1983 are medians.

Note: The years in this table represent the years the data was collected for, not the years in the book titles.

Source: NAHB

Construction Cost Surveys

In addition to *The Cost of Doing Business Study* surveys, NAHB periodically conducts a construction cost survey asking builders to break down costs and expenses of their typical home as follows: finished lot cost, construction costs, financing costs, overhead and general expenses, marketing costs, sales commissions, and profits. The data are national averages because the sample size does not allow for regional breakdowns. Although they are not a perfect tool for estimating the costs of a particular house, the results can provide a broad idea of construction costs for a typical home. Table 9.2 summarizes the results through 2019, the last time NAHB conducted the survey. A full article on the findings is available on NAHB's website.

According to the 2019 results, about 18.5% of a typical home's sales price pays for the finished lot, which includes raw land and development costs. Construction costs (labor, materials, and subcontractors) account for more than half the price of a home, at 61.1%, while overhead and general expenses take up 4.9%, sales commissions 3.7%, financing costs 1.7%, and marketing costs 1.0%. In the end, only 9.1% of the typical home's sales price goes to pre-tax profits.

When reading the data in tables 9.1 and 9.2, it is important to keep in mind that results from *The Cost of Doing Business Study* (table 9.1) are based on company-wide operations, so the percentages are of total revenue spent on expenses from all operations combined. Data from the Construction Cost survey (table 9.2), on the other hand, are based on builders' estimates of how the price of an individual home is allocated among various categories, so the numbers there represent percentages of an average home's price, not of total company revenue. It is also important to mention that the Construction Cost results shown in table 9.2 are based on surveys that do not control for the characteristics of the homes sampled, and so the data on prices, square footage, and lot size may change from one survey to the next in ways that do not reflect overall national trends.

Table 9.2. Cost breakdown of single-family home (% of sales price)

	1995	1998	2002	2004	2007	2009	2011	2013	2015	2017	2019
Finished Lot Cost	24.4	23.6	23.5	26.0	24.5	20.3	21.7	18.6	18.2	21.5	18.5
Total Construction Cost	53.3	54.8	50.8	51.7	48.1	58.9	59.3	61.7	61.8	55.6	61.1
Financing Cost	2.0	1.9	2.1	1.8	2.4	1.7	2.1	1.4	1.3	1.8	1.7
Overhead & General Expenses	5.8	5.7	5.5	5.8	7.0	5.4	5.2	4.3	5.6	5.1	4.9
Marketing Cost	2.2	1.4	2.4	1.9	2.5	1.4	1.5	1.1	0.8	1.2	1.0
Sales Commission	3.3	3.4	3.7	3.0	4.3	3.4	3.3	3.6	3.2	4.1	3.7
Profit	9.1	9.2	12.0	9.8	11.2	8.9	6.8	9.3	9.0	10.7	9.1
Total	**100.0**	**100.0**	**100.0**	**100.0**	**100.0**	**100.0**	**100.0**	**100.0**	**100.0**	**100.0**	**100.0**
Sales Price	**$183,585**	**$226,680**	**$298,412**	**$373,349**	**$454,906**	**$377,624**	**$310,619**	**$399,532**	**$468,318**	**$427,892**	**$485,128**

Source: NAHB Surveys of Builder Members

Note: 2002 data based on survey of builder members carried out in late 2002-early 2003.

Public Firms

The financial reports of publicly traded home building companies offer another view of profitability in the construction industry. Table 9.3 shows revenue, as well as pretax and post-tax profits for 12 public builders for 2014, 2017, and 2020[3]. When aggregated, they earned total revenue of $94.5 billion in 2020, almost 40% more than in 2017 ($67.8 billion), and more than twice the revenue in 2014 ($43.5 billion).

All public builders in table 9.3 posted positive pretax profits for fiscal year 2020. Lennar reported the highest pre-tax profits that year, at $3.1 billion. Altogether, this group's pre-tax profits reached $12.6 billion, 73% higher than in 2017 ($7.3 billion), and an impressive 160% higher than in 2014 ($4.9 billion). After paying for corporate taxes in 2020, their combined total profit was $9.3 billion, 150% higher than in 2017 ($3.7 billion), and 140% more than in 2014 ($3.9 billion).

Under pre-2018 tax law, all businesses could claim operating losses from previous tax years as a deduction against current year net income, thereby reducing current year tax liability. Losses could be carried forward for up to 20 years. Such claims acted to increase after-tax income for accounting purposes by realizing a previously deferred tax asset as income. In other words, the deferred asset, which had potential future value as a future tax deduction, increased after-tax income when realized.The tax deduction reduced taxable income in the year to which it was carried forward, thus increasing after-tax income by reducing taxes paid.

The Tax Cuts and Jobs Act (TCJA) passed at the end of 2017, however, placed limits on the use of net operating losses so that, starting in tax year 2018, businesses may no longer use them to offset all of their taxable income in subsequent years. In oversimplified terms, the deduction is now limited to 80% of a business' taxable income, it must be applied in the

---

[3] Data provided are for each builder's fiscal year, which does not necessarily correspond to the calendar year.

first tax year in which it has positive taxable income, but may also be carried indefinitely, rather than limited to a 20-year period. For a more thorough understanding of the impact of the TCJA on businesses, visit NAHB Economics Group's blog (EyeOnHousing.org) and look up the tax reform toolkit.

Table 9.3. Twelve publicly traded builders ($ millions)

	2014			2017			2020		
	Revenue	**Pretax Profit**	**After-tax Profit**	**Revenue**	**Pretax Profit**	**After-tax Profit**	**Revenue**	**Pretax Profit**	**After-tax Profit**
D.R. Horton	8,025	814	534	14,091	1,602	1,038	20,311	2,983	2,374
Lennar	7,780	970	639	12,646	1,190	810	22,489	3,124	2,465
Pulte Group	5,697	635	474	8,578	939	447	11,036	1,729	1,407
NVR	4,375	428	282	6,306	847	538	7,537	1,078	901
Taylor Morrison	2,708	566	71	3,885	739	91	6,129	1,044	243
Meritage Homes	2,170	208	142	3,227	248	143	4,482	534	423
KB Homes	2,401	95	918	4,369	290	181	4,183	364	296
Toll Brothers	3,912	505	340	5,815	814	535	6,937	587	447
MDC Holdings	1,695	100	63	2,578	230	142	3,901	458	368
M/I	1,215	253	51	1,962	120	72	3,046	310	240
Hovnanian Enterprises	2,063	20	307	2,452	(45)	(332)	2,344	55	51
Beazer	1,464	263	34	1,916	313	32	2,127	348	52
Total	**43,505**	**4,857**	**3,855**	**67,825**	**7,287**	**3,697**	**94,522**	**12,614**	**9,267**

Pretax profit margins for the same group of builders are shown in table 9.4. On aggregate, their annual 10k reports show an average 12.1% net profit margin for fiscal year 2020, about 2 percentage points higher than in 2017 (10.2%) and just shy of 1 point higher than in 2014 (11.4%). On its worst year, 2008, their combined net loss margin was -25.7%.

Table 9.4. Pretax profit margins for select publicly traded builders (% or revenue)

	2014	2017	2020
D.R. Horton	10.1	11.4	14.7
Lennar	12.5	9.4	13.9
Pulte	11.1	10.9	15.7
NVR	9.8	13.4	14.3
Taylor Morrison	20.9	19.0	17.0
Meritage Homes	9.6	7.7	11.9
KB Homes	4.0	6.6	8.7
Toll Brothers	12.9	14.0	8.5
MDC Holdings	5.9	8.9	11.7
M/I	20.8	6.1	10.2
Hovnanian Enterprises	1.0	-1.8	2.3
Beazer	18.0	16.3	16.4
Average	**11.4**	**10.2**	**12.1**

APPENDIX

I

3 Steps To Speed Up Profitability

Efficiencies you can make today to improve your profitability and strengthen relationships with trade partners.

By Carrie Roeger

A NAHB Professional Women in Building Council Article

"It's crazy out here!" How many times do you hear this from your industry peers?

There are more obstacles and opportunities in our industry today than there have ever been for most of us. Though it may be a crazy time – full of uncontrollable costs, delivery delays, material availability, and even worker shortages – there are things you can control to increase your profitability, if you slow down to speed up.

What does that mean: *Slow down to speed up?* You will need to focus – therefore, *slow down* – on the following suggestions, which can lead to a path of increased profitability. By taking the time to slow down to find and make changes, your organization will be able to speed up through improved efficiencies, which will increase profitability. The opportunities below are some of the only controllable factors we have today.

1. Value Engineer Your Plans.

Don't know how? Gather your team, including your trade partners. Walk your floor plans together and talk about waste. (There are companies you can hire to help you do this as well, but you likely have the talent available already.)

Talk about the way a plan is framed. Are you using the best, most efficient framing techniques? Are there material changes you can make and still meet your quality standards? Can you add or subtract inches from the plan in order to reduce waste and lumber cuts? With each of these changes, you can create a ripple effect of material and labor savings through the build.

If you scrub every aspect of your floor plan with your trades, you will find a plethora of changes that will create savings in material and labor, and will ultimately create a better product. Will this take time? Yes. Are the benefits there? Yes. Slow down to speed up. (A side benefit to hosting this event as a team is you solidify relationships with your trade partners by demonstrating they are valuable to you.)

A functioning, reliable schedule is a keystone in that it impacts so many other aspects of the home building business.

2. Modify Your Scheduling.

Undoubtedly, your current construction schedule looks nothing like it did a year ago. More than likely, schedules are being modified in a reactionary manner to the new information from manufacturers and trades.

What would happen if the entire team were to come together and map out the construction schedule on the whiteboard? The bottlenecks will become apparent, wasted days will show themselves, and solutions will be identified. Devising a new schedule with flexibility can assist not only the builder company but the trades as well. A functioning, reliable schedule is a keystone in that it impacts so many other aspects of the home building business.

3. Manage Your Business Through Key Performance Indicators (KPIs).

KPIs create accountability tools for the team, as well as provide leading (predictive) indicators for success. These indicators should be built around metrics and milestones that move your organization to its established goals. Measuring the right performance metrics will create opportunities to improve results on a daily, weekly or even monthly basis. It may seem you can't *slow down* to focus on metrics of success, but you will find that you can *speed up* if you measure the right things.

Although survival may be possible in a world of reactionary decisions, smart organizations take the time to *slow down,* and do the work of making improvements to plans, schedules and measurements in order to *speed up* and increase profitability. Take the time today and reap the rewards tomorrow.

Where does your team need to *slow down?* How can you carve out the time to tackle these three opportunities? Pick one thing and start this week.

Carrie Roeger began her career in a builder organization focused on active adult homebuilding, Carrie gained experience in corporate positions, including Purchasing, Marketing, and Operations, throughout her 15-year tenure with the company.

With this experience, Carrie has created sales, marketing, and strategic plans that allow continued success, regardless of economic or competitive influences. Now owner of White Stone Residential, Carrie builds homes in the West Georgia market.

Carrie spent five years on active duty with the United States Marine Corps. She earned her Finance Degree at UNC-Wilmington and an Executive MBA from the Jack Welch Management Institute. Carrie is the 2021 Chair and a member of the National Association of Homebuilders 55+ Housing Council.carrie@whitestoneresidential.com or 404-606-5417.

APPENDIX

II

Understanding Your Income Statement

By Steven W. Hays, Sr., CPA

An income statement is one of the most important tools for measuring a company's financial operating performance. This financial report summarizes revenues and expenses (in this case, costs of construction and operating expenses) and reflects the "bottom line." The resulting net profit (or loss) is then included in the company's retained earnings or net worth.

This report ultimately measures a company's economic performance in "cost basis" numbers. Successful builders understand the importance of managing and monitoring their income statements.

Income Statement Elements

A "standard" home builder's income statement, as classified by NAHB's Chart of Accounts (available to NAHB members online at www.nahb.org/chart), consists of the following categories:

Sales: all revenue generated from sales.

Developed lot costs: the cost of the raw land and related development costs that result in a developed lot.

Direct construction costs: known as "sticks and bricks," these arc the major costs incurred in the construction of a new home. These costs can always be traced to a particular project and unit of construction.

Indirect construction costs: other construction costs that cannot be easily and directly charged to a specific unit of construction.

Total costs of construction: the sum of developed lot costs, plus direct construction costs, plus indirect construction costs.

Gross profit: sales minus the cost of goods sold (or construction).

Financial costs: interest and other costs related to construction or development financing.

Selling expenses: sales salaries and commissions, advertising, and model home expenses.

General and administrative expenses: all "overhead" costs, including owner's compensation.

Total operating expenses: the sum of financial costs, plus selling expenses, plus general and administrative expenses.

Net profit (loss) before income taxes: literally the "bottom line" of an income statement.

Why Study an Income Statement?

Structuring an income statement according to NAHB's Chart of Accounts categories allows a home builders to better compare their company's financial performance against industry standards. When financial data is consistently classified into these categories, builders can compute meaningful financial ratios.

Financial ratios are important because they help builders understand how their company makes money, identify areas that require attention or different resources, and comprehend key financial ratios that are important to lenders (particularly debt-to-equity ratio and various returns on assets and sales).

For example, a builder can compute operating ratios by comparing the various costs and expenses on an income statement with the closed volume (sales) that also appears on the statement. The builder can then compare those operating ratios to industry operating ratios or to those of other builders.

Comparing operating ratios to industry ratios may inspire a builder to capitalize on favorable results, analyze future potential, or make changes based on unfavorable comparisons. Performing this type of financial analysis can help business owners improve their operating performance. Here are two important items to calculate and monitor:

- **Gross profit analysis.** The gross profit percentage (which consists of sales minus costs of construction) is a key financial measure. It represents a builder's ability to cover or absorb other operating expenses. If a builder cannot maintain an adequate gross profit margin, it's unlikely he or she can obtain an acceptable net profit. Maintaining an acceptable gross profit margin is essential to long-term economic viability.

- **Direct construction costs as a percentage of sales.** Managing this number is critical. Direct construction costs are the largest cost a home builder incurs, yet some builders do very little to control these costs. A common characteristic of successful builders is their ability to monitor and manage direct construction costs. Even a small reduction in direct construction costs as a percentage of the sales price can significantly increase a builder's bottom line. Any costs that can be removed or decreased from a house and multiplied with direct construction cost savings from other units can provide substantial income improvement.

At a minimum, income statements should be prepared and reviewed monthly and annually (the latter would show year-to-date figures). Results should be compared to similar periods from the prior year and to the current year's budget.

The budget should be structured to display historical data in the same manner as the income statement in order to facilitate ease of comparing the documents, analyze the results, and making changes where necessary.

Understanding your income statement will make a significant difference in achieving higher profits and growth. Monitoring key ratios generated from the income statement will allow management to make better decisions. These ratios can help you determine, among other things. Successful product lines and optimum staffing levels.

Steven Hays is Partner-In-Charge of the Home Builders Services Group RubinBrown LLP, Certified Public Accountants in St. Louis, Mo. RubinBrown provides accounting, tax, and business consulting services to more than 40 home building groups primarily in the Midwest. Steven can be reached at 314-290-3336 or steve.hays@rubinhrown.com.

APPENDIX

III

Is Your Job Site Safe . . . Or Just Lucky?

Even if it's your trade contractor's mistake, OSHA may hold you responsible

By Joyce Duerfeldt

In 2018, 20% of the 5,250 worker fatalities in private industry were in construction. That's one out of five worker deaths.

If one of your job sites were visited today by a Compliance Safety and Health Officer (CSHO) from the Occupational Safety and Health Administration (OSHA), due to an accident, complaint, drive by, or random selection, would it qualify for a "focused inspection?" Or would it be subject to a "comprehensive inspection?"

The CSHO will be looking for violations and potential hazards. If your company has (1) an effective written safety program and (2) a designated competent person responsible for and capable of implementing your safety program, then your job site may be eligible to have a "focused inspection." That's great, because the inspection will concentrate on looking for violations associated with the four main safety hazards that cause approximately 59% of workplace deaths and injuries in residential construction.

These were the Focus Four hazards in 2018 and 2019:

- Falls – the No. 1 cause of death in the construction industry with 338 out of the 1008 total deaths in construction (34%)
- Electrocution – 112 deaths (11%)
- Struck-By – 86 deaths (9%)
- Caught-in between – 55 deaths (6%)

Eliminating these four hazards would save 591 workers' lives each year.

The CSHO determines which projects are eligible for focused inspections. On job sites where OSHA determines that there is *inadequate* contractor commitment to safety and health, a comprehensive, resource-intensive inspection will be made. In other words, the latter group of employers will receive OSHA's full attention.

An effective safety and health program starts at the top, with management commitment to a "zero-accident" goal that begins with the owner of the company and is embraced by all of its employees. Having a written safety and health program is the next step. The program should explain the company's commitment to safety and how employees and trade partners are both responsible for integrating safety into every aspect of their jobs.

As builders, most of us have very few of our own employees on our job sites, so why do we need to be concerned about compliance with OSHA Standards for the Construction Industry?

OSHA holds accountable not only the employer who has exposed his or her employees to unsafe conditions, but also the employer who has overall site safety responsibility (usually the builder), as well as the employer who may have caused the unsafe conditions. As the builder, you are responsible for safe working conditions for everyone on your job site — employees, trade partner employees, vendors, customers, and invited visitors. For a single violation, multiple citations may be issued to:

- Creating employer – that caused a hazardous condition
- Exposing employer – whose own employees are exposed to the hazard
- Correcting employer – responsible for correcting a hazard
- Controlling employer – which usually is the builder in charge of the job

Simply stated, a builder may also receive a citation for a violation created by a trade partner, whether or not the builder caused the hazard or even knew about the hazard.

Many small building companies wrongly believe that implementing a safety program is too difficult or too time consuming. Perhaps this is why small-volume builders are the source of most of the fatalities in residential construction.

Within the past seven years, 15% of the fall, scaffold, or overhead power line fatalities occurred on weekends. For years, half of the fatalities occurred on Saturdays. As a result, OSHA is now randomly conducting inspections of construction sites operating on weekends.

Job site safety is not just about avoiding a citation from OSHA. It's about avoiding hazards. It's about making sure that you have an effective safety program within your company — no matter how big or small it may be. It's about ensuring that your superintendents and construction managers are maintaining a safe, clean jobsite, and that all your trade contractors and vendors use safe work practices. And finally, it's about sending everyone home at the end of the workday to their families, safe and injury free.

As we found out in 2020 from the COVID pandemic, other disaster readiness challenges can see OSHA and its affiliates play a role. Builder and contractor readiness can start with online resources from NAHB on the Coronavirus Response and Recovery.

One thing to keep in mind is how such disasters may see guidelines published before rules, yet those guidelines may see enforcement under emergency measures. We learned that visible compliance is key to our industry's credibility. Don't be the contractor with an easy to photograph non-compliant job site. With social media and plenty of public interest, non-compliance can result in a social media nightmare that may not allow the industry an "essential" designation next time. Be sure to understand any emergency rules and that they are enforced at your employer level.

As with any safety challenge, a pandemic, a flood, or the like, may require short term expense and effort to allow for ongoing business operations. Overreaction is to be avoided and substituted for with calm research and understanding. Clear communications to employees and subcontractors as to the facts, the additional safety measures and the consequences of non-compliance need to be reiterated frequently and updated as guidelines change.

Good examples of professional builders who are serious about safety can be found around the country. For example, Alan Banks, a builder from Charlotte, N.C., who serves as a member of NAHB'S Construction Health and Safety Committee, gave great insight into his company's Safety Culture.

> "Safety is intangible, while our construction industry is surrounded by tangibles like lumber, drywall, labor, and land. You have to think of safety as something else you bring to the site to build a home."
>
> "Safety, to us, has to be like another trade partner on the site. Just like lumber or a drywall trade partner, safety has to show up. Making safety less of a concept and more of a real thing has helped make the point and make safety a priority. If safety is at the job site, usually everything goes fine. If safety doesn't show up, we all notice."
>
> "Safety in our culture has no predefined fixed or variable cost. The absence of safety, though, has real and unpredictable costs."

NAHB and HBI have worked with OSHA on various safety resources. For more information visit the Construction Safety and Health Committee web page for ready to use documents, videos, and more to further your safety efforts.

You can find the *NAHB Jobsite Safety Handbook, English-Spanish, Fourth Edition* along with other books at NAHB BuilderBooks.

Joyce Duerfeldt currently serves on NAHB'S Business Management and Information Technology committee. She is a member of the Spokane Home Builders Association and has been in key leadership roles with the Professional Women in Building Council. Joyce serves in administrative and marketing roles with NWCALLIANCE with her husband Treacy.

APPENDIX

IV

2021 Builders' Cost of Doing Business Survey

I. FIRM'S PROFILE

1. Indicate your firm's main operation during fiscal year 2020 and write in the percentage of your business that operation represents.

	Main operation (Check ONE only)	Percent of Your Business
Single-family production builder	☐	_______ %
Single-family custom builder (on owner's lot)	☐	_______ %
Single-family custom builder (on builder's lot)	☐	_______ %
Multifamily builder (condo/co-op units)	☐	_______ %
Multifamily builder (for-rent units)	☐	_______ %
Land developer	☐	_______ %
Residential remodeling/rehabilitation	☐	_______ %
Other (specify)	☐	_______ %
	Total:	**100%**

2. How many years has your firm been in the residential construction business? ________year(s)

3. Of the total number of single family-units your firm closed in fiscal year 2020, how many were pre-sold, speculative, and/or built on others' land (owners' lots)? *(If none in a category, please write zero.)*

	Single-Family Units Closed
Pre-sold (on builder's lot)	__________
Speculative	__________
Built on others' land (owners' lots)	__________
TOTAL	__________

II. FINANCIAL INFORMATION

4. Balance Sheet for fiscal year 2020.

Each code number refers to the NAHB Chart of Accounts, found at www.nahb.org/chart]			
Assets		**Liabilities and Owner's Equity**	
Cash [1000-1090]	$	Current Liabilities [2000-2490]	$
Receivables and Inventories [1200-1390]	$	Construction Loans Payable [2230]	$
Construction Work in Progress [1400-1490]	$	Long-term Loans Payable [2510, 2530]	$
Other Current Assets [1500-1690]	$	Other Long-Term Liabilities [2600-2890]	
Other Assets [1700-1990]	$	Owner's Equity [2900-2990]	$
Total Assets	$	Total Liabilities and Owner's Equity	$

Note: Total assets must equal the total of liabilities plus owner's equity.

5. Income Statement for fiscal year 2020.

* Each code number refers to the NAHB Chart of Accounts, found at www.nahb.org/chart		
Revenue from Operations		
Single-family Home Building [3100-3125]	$	
Residential Remodeling Revenue [3130]	$	
Multifamily Revenue [3140]	$	
Light Commercial/Industrial Revenue [3150]	$	
All Other Revenue [3000, 3050, 3160-3490]	$	
Total Company Revenue [sum of the previous five entries]		$
Cost of Sales		
Land Costs [3550]	$	
Single-family Home Building Direct Construction Costs [3600, 3610, 3620,3625] (permits, labor with burden, trade contractors, material costs, other unit-specific construction cost)	$	
Residential Remodeling Direct Construction Cost [3800-3899]	$	
Multifamily Direct Construction Costs [3640]	$	
Light Commercial/Industrial Direct Construction Costs [3650]	$	
Indirect Construction Costs [4000-4990] (job site and non-unit specific construction costs; include job supervision, estimating, purchasing and design personnel, warranty costs, construction vehicles, tools, and any other indirect costs)	$	
All Other Cost of Goods Sold (cost of sales related to items that fall under "All Other Revenue")	$	
Total Company Cost of Sales [sum of previous seven entries]		$
Gross Profit		
Total Company Revenue less Total Company Cost of Sales		$
Operating Expenses		
Financing Expenses [5000-5990] (points and interest on all loans)	$	
Sales and Marketing Expenses [6000-6990] (commissions, sales salaries and burden, advertising and sales promotion, and model home maintenance)	$	
General and Administrative Expenses [8000-8790; 8900-8990] (salaries, payroll taxes, and benefits of non job-related personnel; office & computer expenses, vehicles, travel, entertainment, taxes, insurance, professional services) (exclude owner's compensation)	$	
Depreciation [8800-8890]	$	
Owner's Compensation [8010] (owner's salary, draws, bonuses and benefits)	$	
Total Operating Expenses [sum of previous five entries]		$
Net Income Before Taxes [total company gross profit minus total operating expenses]		$

APPENDIX

V

Detailed Tables

Appendix V

V.1. Cost of Doing Business Study detailed tables

Q1. Indicate your Firm's Main Operation During Fiscal year 2020
(Percent of Respondents)

	Total	Region				Total 2020 Revenue ($ millions)			Number of Homes Closed				Type of Builder		
		Northeast	Midwest	South	West	<2	2-9.9	≥10	<10	10-25	26-99	≥100	With land costs	Without land costs	Combination
Single-family production builder	26	28	17	25	38	18	23	70	9	23	59	86	46	2	23
Single-family custom builder (on owner's lot)	39	40	38	42	28	50	61	15	61	39	12	10	13	94	44
Single-family custom builder (on builder's lot)	25	19	29	26	20	32	16	15	29	38	29	3	41	4	32
Multifamily builder (condo/co-op units)	1		1	0	3										
Multifamily builder (for-rent units)	1	4	1	1	2										
Land Developer	1		1	1											
Residential remodeling/rehabilitation	6	6	10	4	5										
Other	1	2	1	1	3										

Q1b. Percent of your business from each operation
(Average Share)

	Total	Region				Total 2020 Revenue ($ millions)			Number of Homes Closed				Type of Builder		
		Northeast	Midwest	South	West	<2	2-9.9	≥10	<10	10-25	26-99	≥100	With land costs	Without land costs	Combination
Single-family production builder	23	26	16	23	33	13	15	62	9	20	51	78	40	2	21
Single-family custom builder (on owner's lot)	34	31	34	37	25	38	47	14	48	36	15	12	14	71	39
Single-family custom builder (on builder's lot)	25	21	27	26	20	36	22	12	30	35	25	3	37	8	32
Multifamily builder (condo/co-op units)	2	2	3	1	3	0	1	0	1	1	2	1	2	1	2
Multifamily builder (for-rent units)	2	6	1	1	3	2	0	4	0	0	2	1	1	1	0
Land Developer	3	2	3	2	5	2	4	4	1	3	3	5	4	0	2
Residential remodeling/rehabilitation	9	9	13	8	9	9	8	2	9	4	1	0	2	15	4
Other	2	3	2	1	4	1	2	1	1	0	0	0	0	2	0

V.1. Cost of Doing Business Study detailed tables *(continued)*

Q2. Years Firm Has Been in Residential Construction Business
(Percent of Respondents)

	Total	Region				Total 2020 Revenue ($ millions)			Number of Homes Closed				Type of Builder		
		Northeast	Midwest	South	West	<2	2-9.9	≥10	<10	10-25	26-99	≥100	With land costs	Without land costs	Combination
Under 5 years	4		2	5	5	23			8	4			5	9	3
5-10 years	14	13	11	15	16	23	10	6	17	16	16	7	17	11	16
11-19 years	21	13	22	22	21	23	33	27	21	20	23	32	17	23	25
20-29 years	22	8	20	23	25	9	20	27	22	23	20	36	28	22	18
30+ Years	39	66	46	34	34	23	37	39	33	38	41	25	32	35	38
Average (Years)	25	32	30	24	23	17	25	27	23	25	26	26	25	24	24
Median (Years)	23	34	26	21	21	13	22	26	20	23	25	23	23	21	21

Q3. Of single-family units closed in 2020, indicate how many were pre-sold, speculative, and/or built on other's (owner's) land?
(Average number of homes closed)

	Total	Region				Total 2020 Revenue ($ millions)			Number of Homes Closed				Type of Builder		
		Northeast	Midwest	South	West	<2	2-9.9	≥10	<10	10-25	26-99	≥100	With land costs	Without land costs	Combination
Pre-Sold -on Builders lot	14	12	14	14	20	1	5	46	1	6	30	106	23	0	14
Speculative	7	5	7	7	9	2	4	14	1	5	16	39	13	0	6
Built on other's land -owner's lots	5	3	4	5	3	1	7	5	3	5	7	11	0	7	7
Total	26	20	25	26	32	4	15	65	5	15	53	156	36	7	26

V.1. Cost of Doing Business Study detailed tables *(continued)*

Q4. Balance Sheet
(Average in $1,000s)

	Total	Region				Total 2020 Revenue ($ millions)			Number of Homes Closed				Type of Builder		
		Northeast	Midwest	South	West	<2	2-9.9	≥10	<10	10-25	26-99	≥100	With land costs	Without land costs	Combination
ASSETS															
Cash	1,235		931	1,160	1,724	185	341	1,961	222	506	2,085	2,525	1,189	294	1,307
Receivables and Inventories	850		967	779	719	71	137	1,884	144	507	1,760	905	451	464	1,158
Construction Work in Progress	5,891		3,319	6,852	6,660	418	1,240	10,423	1,383	4,023	6,069	18,602	6,546	4,344	5,355
Other Current Assets	571		628	382	689	33	435	741	168	409	505	1,224	453	133	630
Other Assets	894		1,459	820	708	21	350	609	46	192	957	2,974	823	148	871
Total Assets	9,441		7,304	9,993	10,501	729	2,502	15,618	1,964	5,637	11,375	26,230	9,463	5,383	9,321
LIABILITIES															
Current Liabilities	2,921		4,370	2,797	2,158	209	899	2,938	856	1,066	1,708	11,209	2,985	1,433	2,656
Construction Loans Payable	2,356		792	2,044	4,490	234	693	4,582	410	1,406	3,573	3,598	2,344	4	2,352
Long-term Loans Payable	680		642	927	240	66	177	1,546	65	132	608	3,726	1,117	58	634
Other Long-Term Liabilities	112		154	99	114	20	92	186	20	47	152	427	80	3	209
Owner's Equity	3,373		1,347	4,126	3,498	201	641	6,367	613	2,985	5,335	7,270	2,938	3,884	3,470
Total Liabilities and Owner's Equity	9,441		7,304	9,993	10,501	729	2,502	15,618	1,964	5,637	11,375	26,230	9,463	5,383	9,321

V.1. Cost of Doing Business Study detailed tables *(continued)*

Q5. Income Statement

(Average in $1,000s)

	Total	Region				Total 2020 Revenue			Number of Homes Closed				Type of Builder		
		Northeast	Midwest	South	West	<2	2-9.9	≥10	<10	10-25	26-99	≥100	With land costs	Without land costs	Combination
Revenue															
Single-Family home building	12,854		13,682	11,422	17,322	975	4,412	28,702	2,261	7,967	21,378	43,236	14,044	6,223	14,730
Residential Remodeling	344		541	353	37	60	299	575	334	824	5	48	44	1,370	197
Multifamily home building	110		384	68	16	51	0	252	10	341	145	0	-	420	116
Light Commercial/Industrial	152		372	160	2	25	51	333	65	399	0	-	1	664	-
All Other Revenue	243		56	313	235	6	186	454	44	116	199	223	125	14	168
Total Company Revenue	13,702		15,034	12,316	17,612	1,117	4,948	30,316	2,713	9,647	21,727	43,507	14,214	8,692	15,211
Cost of Sales															
Land Costs	1,784		1,889	1,480	2,471	100	452	4,158	210	530	3,679	5,649	2,523	0	1,603
Single-family home building Direct Construction Costs	8,242		9,026	7,272	11,147	705	3,271	17,936	1,686	6,429	12,318	27,410	8,378	5,414	9,707
Residential Remodeling Direct Construction Costs	447		397	635	27	46	240	909	256	610	979	95	29	1,091	716
Multifamily Direct Construction Costs	84		279	61	1	1	0	217	1	271	109	0	-	363	65
Light Commercial/Industrial Direct Construction Costs	154		365	161	13	31	64	321	82	383	0	-	1	636	24
Indirect Construction Costs	384		424	357	430	51	128	846	75	153	556	1,651	537	43	399
All other Cost of Goods Sold	118		8	171	56	2	35	274	5	1	15	2	9	0	5
Total Company Cost of Sales	11,212		12,388	10,137	14,145	935	4,189	24,662	2,315	8,377	17,654	34,808	11,476	7,548	12,519
Gross Profit	**2,490**		**2,646**	**2,179**	**3,466**	**182**	**759**	**5,654**	**398**	**1,269**	**4,073**	**8,699**	**2,738**	**1,143**	**2,692**
Operating Expenses															
Financing Expenses	178		200	102	394	13	56	404	19	71	391	576	253	3	186
Sales and Marketing Expenses	556		636	460	832	20	97	1,345	23	150	888	2,514	744	27	576
General and Administrative Expenses	597		730	514	692	73	252	1,270	121	434	881	2,047	678	396	589
Depreciation	20		28	13	18	1	22	30	4	25	36	21	6	22	33
Owner's Compensation	180		167	212	113	60	148	290	113	244	256	154	115	301	206
Total Operating Expenses	1,531		1,760	1,300	2,049	167	574	3,338	280	924	2,452	5,310	1,795	748	1,590
Net Income Before Taxes	**959**		**886**	**878**	**1,417**	**15**	**185**	**2,316**	**118**	**345**	**1,621**	**3,389**	**943**	**395**	**1,102**

V.1. Cost of Doing Business Study detailed tables *(continued)*

Q5. Income Statement

(% Share of Revenue)

	Total	Region				Total 2017 Revenue			Number of Homes Closed				Type of Builder		
		Northeast	Midwest	South	West	<2	2-9.9	≥10	<10	10-25	26-99	≥100	With land costs	Without land costs	Combination
Revenue															
Single-Family home building	93.8		91.0	92.7	98.4	87.3	89.2	94.7	83.3	82.6	98.4	99.4	98.8	71.6	96.8
Residential Remodeling	2.5		3.6	2.9	0.2	5.4	6.0	1.9	12.3	8.5	0.0	0.1	0.3	15.8	1.3
Multifamily home building	0.8		2.6	0.6	0.1	4.5	0.0	0.8	0.4	3.5	0.7	0.0	0.0	4.8	0.8
Light Commercial/Industrial	1.1		2.5	1.3	0.0	2.2	1.0	1.1	2.4	4.1	0.0	0.0	0.0	7.6	0.0
All Other Revenue	1.8		0.4	2.5	1.3	0.6	3.8	1.5	1.6	1.2	0.9	0.5	0.9	0.2	1.1
Total Company Revenue	100.0		100.0	100.0	100.0	100.0	100.0	100.0	100.0	100.0	100.0	100.0	100.0	100.0	100.0
Cost of Sales															
Land Costs	13.0		12.6	12.0	14.0	8.9	9.1	13.7	7.7	5.5	16.9	13.0	17.8	0.0	10.5
Single-family home building Direct Construction Costs	60.1		60.0	59.0	63.3	63.1	66.1	59.2	62.1	66.6	56.7	63.0	58.9	62.3	63.8
Residential Remodeling Direct Construction Costs	3.3		2.6	5.2	0.2	4.1	4.8	3.0	9.4	6.3	4.5	0.2	0.2	12.6	4.7
Multifamily Direct Construction Costs	0.6		1.9	0.5	0.0	0.1	0.0	0.7	0.0	2.8	0.5	0.0	0.0	4.2	0.4
Light Commercial/Industrial Direct Construction Costs	1.1		2.4	1.3	0.1	2.7	1.3	1.1	3.0	4.0	0.0	0.0	0.0	7.3	0.2
Indirect Construction Costs	2.8		2.8	2.9	2.4	4.6	2.6	2.8	2.8	1.6	2.6	3.8	3.8	0.5	2.6
All other Cost of Goods Sold	0.9		0.1	1.4	0.3	0.2	0.7	0.9	0.2	0.0	0.1	0.0	0.1	0.0	0.0
Total Company Cost of Sales	81.8		82.4	82.3	80.3	83.7	84.7	81.3	85.3	86.8	81.3	80.0	80.7	86.8	82.3
Gross Profit	**18.2**		**17.6**	**17.7**	**19.7**	**16.3**	**15.3**	**18.7**	**14.7**	**13.2**	**18.7**	**20.0**	**19.3**	**13.2**	**17.7**
Operating Expenses															
Financing Expenses	1.3		1.3	0.8	2.2	1.2	1.1	1.3	0.7	0.7	1.8	1.3	1.8	0.0	1.2
Sales and Marketing Expenses	4.1		4.2	3.7	4.7	1.8	2.0	4.4	0.8	1.6	4.1	5.8	5.2	0.3	3.8
General and Administrative Expenses	4.4		4.9	4.2	3.9	6.5	5.1	4.2	4.4	4.5	4.1	4.7	4.8	4.6	3.9
Depreciation	0.1		0.2	0.1	0.1	0.1	0.4	0.1	0.2	0.3	0.2	0.0	0.0	0.2	0.2
Owner's Compensation	1.3		1.1	1.7	0.6	5.4	3.0	1.0	4.2	2.5	1.2	0.4	0.8	3.5	1.4
Total Operating Expenses	11.2		11.7	10.6	11.6	15.0	11.6	11.0	10.3	9.6	11.3	12.2	12.6	8.6	10.5
Net Income Before Taxes	**7.0**		**5.9**	**7.1**	**8.0**	**1.4**	**3.7**	**7.6**	**4.4**	**3.6**	**7.5**	**7.8**	**6.6**	**4.5**	**7.2**

V.2. All single-family builders

Top 25% and bottom 25% by net profit margin
Income statement
(average in $1,000s)

	ALL	Top 25%	Bottom 25%
Revenue			
Single-Family home building	12,854	15,425	3,071
Residential Remodeling	344	199	321
Multifamily	110	0	39
Light Commercial/Industrial	152	0	29
All Other Revenue	243	591	212
Total Revenue	13,702	16,214	3,671
Costs of Sales			
Land Costs	1,784	2,137	330
Single-family home building Direct Construction Costs	8,242	9,299	2,574
Residential Remodeling Direct Construction Costs	447	156	256
Multifamily Direct Construction Costs	84	0	0
Light Commercial/Industrial Direct Construction Costs	154	0	24
Indirect Construction Costs	384	398	103
All other Costs of Goods Sold	118	384	50
Total Cost of Sales	11,212	12,374	3,338
Gross Profit	**2,490**	**3,840**	**333**
Operating Expenses			
Financing Expense	178	234	49
Sales and Marketing Expense	556	743	46
General and Administrative Expense	597	633	205
Depreciation	20	22	20
Owner's Compensation	180	201	113
Total Operating Expenses	1,531	1,833	433
Net Income Before Taxes	**959**	**2,008**	**(100)**

V.2. All single-family builders

Top 25% and bottom 25% by net profit margin
Income statement
(% share of revenue)

	ALL	Top 25%	Bottom 25%
Revenue			
Single-Family home building	93.8	95.1	83.6
Residential Remodeling	2.5	1.2	8.7
Multifamily	0.8	0.0	1.1
Light Commercial/Industrial	1.1	0.0	0.8
All Other Revenue	1.8	3.6	5.8
Total Revenue	100.0	100.0	100.0
Costs of Sales			
Land Costs	13.0	13.2	9.0
Single-faily home building Direct Construction Costs	60.1	57.4	70.1
Residential Remodeling Direct Construction Costs	3.3	1.0	7.0
Multifamily Direct Construction Costs	0.6	0.0	0.0
Light Commercial/Industrial Direct Construction Costs	1.1	0.0	0.7
Indirect Construction Costs	2.8	2.5	2.8
All other Costs of Goods Sold	0.9	2.4	1.4
Total Cost of Sales	81.8	76.3	90.9
Gross Profit	**18.2**	**23.7**	**9.1**
Operating Expenses			
Financing Expense	1.3	1.4	1.3
Sales and Marketing Expense	4.1	4.6	1.3
General and Administrative Expense	4.4	3.9	5.6
Owner's Compensation	1.3	1.2	3.1
Total Operating Expenses	11.2	11.3	11.8
Net Income Before Taxes	**7.0**	**12.4**	**(2.7)**

Balance Sheet
(Average in $1,000s)

	ALL	Top 25%	Bottom 25%
ASSETS			
Cash	1,235	1,184	300
Receivables and Inventories	850	287	165
Construction Work in Progress	5,891	6,011	1,641
Other Current assets	571	763	106
Other Assets	894	293	270
Total Assets	9,441	8,538	2,482
LIABILITIES			
Current Liabilities	2,921	1,792	687
Construction Loans Payable	2,356	2,005	1,122
Long-Term Loans Payable	680	1,548	207
Other Long-Term Liabilities	112	53	142
Owner's Equity	3,373	3,141	324
Total Liabilities and Owner's Equity	9,441	8,538	2,482

V.3. All single-family builders

Small-volume vs. production builders*

Income statement (average in $1,000s)

	ALL	Small-Volume	Production
Revenue			
Single-Family home building	12,854	4,499	29,247
Residential Remodeling	344	526	21
Multifamily	110	140	93
Light Commercial/Industrial	152	196	0
All Other Revenue	243	72	207
Total Revenue	13,702	5,432	29,568
Costs of Sales			
Land Costs	1,784	335	4,388
Single-family home building Direct Construction Costs	8,242	3,546	17,751
Residential Remodeling Direct Construction Costs	447	395	661
Multifamily Direct Construction Costs	84	107	70
Light Commercial/Industrial Direct Construction Costs	154	200	0
Indirect Construction Costs	384	106	950
All other Costs of Goods Sold	118	4	10
Total Cost of Sales	11,212	4,693	23,830
Gross Profit	**2,490**	**740**	**5,738**
Operating Expenses			
Financing Expense	178	39	457
Sales and Marketing Expense	556	73	1,473
General and Administrative Expense	597	244	1,301
Depreciation	20	12	30
Owner's Compensation	180	165	219
Total Operating Expenses	1,531	533	3,481
Net Income Before Taxes	**959**	**207**	**2,257**

** Small-volume builders closed on 25 or fewer homes in 2020. Production builders closed on 26 or more homes.*

V.3. All single-family builders

Small-volume vs. production builders*

Income statement (% share of revenue)

	ALL	Small-Volume	Production
Revenue			
Single-Family home building	93.8	82.8	98.9
Residential Remodeling	2.5	9.7	0.1
Multifamily	0.8	2.6	0.3
Light Commercial/Industrial	1.1	3.6	0.0
All Other Revenue	1.8	1.3	0.7
Total Revenue	100.0	100.0	100.0
Costs of Sales			
Land Costs	13.0	6.2	14.8
Single-faily home building Direct Construction Costs	60.1	65.3	60.0
Residential Remodeling Direct Construction Costs	3.3	7.3	2.2
Multifamily Direct Construction Costs	0.6	2.0	0.2
Light Commercial/Industrial Direct Construction Costs	1.1	3.7	0.0
Indirect Construction Costs	2.8	1.9	3.2
All other Costs of Goods Sold	0.9	0.1	0.0
Total Cost of Sales	81.8	86.4	80.6
Gross Profit	**18.2**	**13.6**	**19.4**
Operating Expenses			
Financing Expense	1.3	0.7	1.5
Sales and Marketing Expense	4.1	1.3	5.0
General and Administrative Expense	4.4	4.5	4.4
Depreciation	0.1	0.2	0.1
Owner's Compensation	1.3	3.0	0.7
Total Operating Expenses	11.2	9.8	11.8
Net Income Before Taxes	**7.0**	**3.8**	**7.6**

Balance sheet (average in $1,000s)

	ALL	Small-Volume	Production
ASSETS			
Cash	1,235	351	2,250
Receivables and Inventories	850	309	1,439
Construction Work in Progress	5,891	2,583	10,769
Other Current assets	571	278	774
Other Assets	894	112	1,713
Total Assets	9,441	3,633	16,946
LIABILITIES			
Current Liabilities	2,921	951	5,271
Construction Loans Payable	2,356	863	3,582
Long-Term Loans Payable	680	95	1,777
Other Long-Term Liabilities	112	33	255
Owner's Equity	3,373	1,691	6,061
Total Liabilities and Owner's Equity	9,441	3,633	16,946

V.4. Single-family builders with land costs

Small-Volume vs Production Builders*

Income Statement
(Average in $1,000s)

	ALL	Small-Volume	Production
Revenue			
Single-Family home building	14,044	2,977	31,071
Residential Remodeling	44	73	0
Multifamily	0	0	0
Light Commercial/Industrial	1	1	0
All Other Revenue	125	116	138
Total Revenue	14,214	3,168	31,209
Costs of Sales			
Land Costs	2,523	641	5,418
Single-family home building Direct Construction Costs	8,378	2,003	18,186
Residential Remodeling Direct Construction Costs	29	48	0
Multifamily Direct Construction Costs	0	0	0
Light Commercial/Industrial Direct Construction Costs	1	1	0
Indirect Construction Costs	537	127	1,167
All other Costs of Goods Sold	9	8	10
Total Cost of Sales	11,476	2,828	24,781
Gross Profit	**2,738**	**340**	**6,428**
Operating Expenses			
Financing Expense	253	66	541
Sales and Marketing Expense	744	76	1,771
General and Administrative Expense	678	79	1,600
Depreciation	6	3	10
Owner's Compensation	115	82	165
Total Operating Expenses	1,795	305	4,087
Net Income Before Taxes	**943**	**34**	**2,340**

** Small-volume builders closed on 25 or fewer homes in 2020. Production builders closed on 26 or more homes.*

V.4. Single-family builders with land costs

Small-Volume vs Production Builders*

Income Statement

(% share of revenue)

	ALL	Small-Volume	Production
Revenue			
Single-Family home building	98.8	94.0	99.6
Residential Remodeling	0.3	2.3	0.0
Multifamily	0.0	0.0	0.0
Light Commercial/Industrial	0.0	0.0	0.0
All Other Revenue	0.9	3.7	0.4
Total Revenue	100.0	100.0	100.0
Costs of Sales			
Land Costs	17.8	20.2	17.4
Single-faily home building Direct Construction Costs	58.9	63.2	58.3
Residential Remodeling Direct Construction Costs	0.2	1.5	0.0
Multifamily Direct Construction Costs	0.0	0.0	0.0
Light Commercial/Industrial Direct Construction Costs	0.0	0.0	0.0
Indirect Construction Costs	3.8	4.0	3.7
All other Costs of Goods Sold	0.1	0.3	0.0
Total Cost of Sales	80.7	89.3	79.4
Gross Profit	**19.3**	**10.7**	**20.6**
Operating Expenses			
Financing Expense	1.8	2.1	1.7
Sales and Marketing Expense	5.2	2.4	5.7
General and Administrative Expense	4.8	2.5	5.1
Depreciation	0.0	0.1	0.0
Owners Compensation	0.8	2.6	0.5
Total Operating Expenses	12.6	9.6	13.1
Net Income Before Taxes	**6.6**	**1.1**	**7.5**

Balance Sheet

(Average in $1,000s)

	ALL	Small-Volume	Production
ASSETS			
Cash	1,189	305	2,239
Receivables and Inventories	451	134	828
Construction Work in Progress	6,546	1,676	12,331
Other Current Assets	453	433	477
Other Assets	823	49	1,742
Total Assets	9,463	2,597	17,616
LIABILITIES			
Current Liabilities	2,985	383	6,075
Construction Loans Payable	2,344	1,250	3,642
Long-term Loans Payable	1,117	152	2,262
Other Long-Term Liabilities	80	32	136
Owner's Equity	2,938	780	5,500
Total Liabilities and Owner's Equity	9,463	2,597	17,616

V.5. Combination single-family builders

Small-Volume vs Production Builders*

Income Statement
(Average in $1,000s)

	ALL	Small-Volume	Production
Revenue			
Single-Family home building	14,730	4,697	27,271
Residential Remodeling	197	320	43
Multifamily	116	55	193
Light Commercial/Industrial	0	0	0
All Other Revenue	168	76	282
Total Revenue	15,211	5,149	27,790
Costs of Sales			
Land Costs	1,603	268	3,272
Single-family home building Direct Construction Costs	9,707	3,649	17,280
Residential Remodeling Direct Construction Costs	716	187	1,376
Multifamily Direct Construction Costs	65	0	145
Light Commercial/Industrial Direct Construction Costs	24	43	0
Indirect Construction Costs	399	147	715
All other Costs of Goods Sold	5	1	11
Total Cost of Sales	12,519	4,295	22,799
Gross Profit	**2,692**	**854**	**4,991**
Operating Expenses			
Financing Expense	186	42	367
Sales and Marketing Expense	576	117	1,150
General and Administrative Expense	589	278	977
Depreciation	33	17	52
Owner's Compensation	206	149	278
Total Operating Expenses	1,590	603	2,824
Net Income Before Taxes	**1,102**	**251**	**2,167**

** Small-volume builders closed on 25 or fewer homes in 2020. Production builders closed on 26 or more homes.*

V.5. Combination single-family builders

Small-Volume vs Production Builders*
Income Statement
(% share of revenue)

	ALL	Small-Volume	Production
Revenue			
Single-Family home building	96.8	91.2	98.1
Residential Remodeling	1.3	6.2	0.2
Multifamily	0.8	1.1	0.7
Light Commercial/Industrial	0.0	0.0	0.0
All Other Revenue	1.1	1.5	1.0
Total Revenue	100.0	100.0	100.0
Costs of Sales			
Land Costs	10.5	5.2	11.8
Single-faily home building Direct Construction Costs	63.8	70.9	62.2
Residential Remodeling Direct Construction Costs	4.7	3.6	5.0
Multifamily Direct Construction Costs	0.4	0.0	0.5
Light Commercial/Industrial Direct Construction Costs	0.2	0.8	0.0
Indirect Construction Costs	2.6	2.9	2.6
All other Costs of Goods Sold	0.0	0.0	0.0
Total Cost of Sales	82.3	83.4	82.0
Gross Profit	**17.7**	**16.6**	**18.0**
Operating Expenses			
Financing Expense	1.2	0.8	1.3
Sales and Marketing Expense	3.8	2.3	4.1
General and Administrative Expense	3.9	5.4	3.5
Depreciation	0.2	0.3	0.2
Owners Compensation	1.4	2.9	1.0
Total Operating Expenses	10.5	11.7	10.2
Net Income Before Taxes	**7.2**	**4.9**	**7.8**

Balance sheet
(average in $1,000s)

	ALL	Small-Volume	Production
ASSETS			
Cash	1,307	458	2,261
Receivables and Inventories	1,158	364	2,051
Construction Work in Progress	5,355	1,931	9,207
Other Current Assets	630	238	1,072
Other Assets	871	148	1,684
Total Assets	9,321	3,139	16,275
LIABILITIES			
Current Liabilities	2,656	1,047	4,467
Construction Loans Payable	2,352	1,312	3,522
Long-term Loans Payable	634	49	1,292
Other Long-Term Liabilities	209	63	374
Owner's Equity	3,470	669	6,621
Total Liabilities and Owner's Equity	9,321	3,139	16,275

Glossary

accounts payable. The amount of money a business owes for products and services purchased on credit.

accounts receivable. The amount of money owed to a business for products and services provided on credit.

assets. Property or items of tangible or intangible value such as accounts receivable, prepaid expenses, and organization costs that a business owns.

balance sheet. A report of the financial condition of an institution that lists the assets, liabilities, and owner's equity at a particular date; sometimes called a "statement of financial position."

builders with land costs. Builders who build only on their own lots.

builders without land costs. Builders who build exclusively on their customers' land.

capital. Money or assets supplied by banks, investors, or owners of a business. The dollar value of assets contributed to a business.

chart of accounts. A list of all accounts, and their assigned account numbers, used in recording financial transactions.

combination builders. Builders who build both speculative/presold homes on their own land and custom homes on their customers' land.

current assets. Assets that could be used up or converted to cash within the next operating cycle of the business, usually one year.

current liabilities. Debts that must be paid within the next operating cycle of a business, usually one year.

current ratio. A liquidity measure that indicates a company's ability to meet its current liabilities. The relationship between current assets and current liabilities calculated by dividing the dollar amount of current assets by the dollar amount of current liabilities.

debt-to-equity ratio. A measure of leverage in a business equal to the amount of long-term debt divided by the amount of equity contributed by the owners.

expense. The necessary payments associated with a period of time that are used to operate a home building business. Expenses reduce revenue. *See also* financing expenses, general expenses, and sales and marketing expenses.

financing expenses. All interest, points, and service charges related to financing construction activities or company purchases; all closing costs, such as points, taxes, fees, and other miscellaneous charges.

financial ratios. Ratios that identify relationships between different classifications in the financial statements to more clearly define a company's financial strength, efficiency of operation, and return on investment.

general and administrative expenses. Expenses that cannot be classified in other expense categories, such as training and education, charitable contributions, and trade association dues.

gross profit on sales. Total revenue minus cost of goods sold, excluding financing, selling, and administrative expenses.

income statement. A report on business operations showing net income or net loss for a fiscal period; sometimes called a "profit and loss statement."

liabilities. Amounts owed to creditors; the claims of creditors to the assets of the business.

liquidity. The capacity to turn assets into cash.

leverage. The degree to which a business uses borrowed money to finance its assets.

loans payable. Long-term liabilities representing obligations of the company which are due over a period of time. Examples include notes payable and mortgages.

net income. The amount of revenue that remains after deducting costs and expenses for a period.

net loss. The amount by which total costs and expenses exceed total revenue.

net sales. The invoice value of sales minus discounts, returns, or allowances.

operating expenses. The cost of transacting normal business operations, excluding cost of goods sold, interest, and taxes.

owner's compensation. The amount of money an owner would make doing similar work for another company as an employee.

owner's equity. Owner's claims to the assets of the business. Assets minus liabilities.

production builder. A home builder with 26 or more closings per year.

production combination builder. A home builder with 26 or more closings per year who builds both speculative/presold homes on his or her own land and custom homes on customers' land.

production builder with land costs. A home builder with 26 or more closings per year who builds only on his or her own lots.

profit. The amount of revenue that remains after deducting costs and expenses for a period of time.

return on equity. Reward for the owners' capital investment.

revenue. Amount collected for goods and services provided; sales.

sales and marketing expenses. All expenses associated with selling homes, such as advertising expenses, inhouse and broker commissions, models, brochures, and signs.

schedule of accounts payable. A list of all creditors in the accounts payable ledger, the balance in each account, and the total amount owed to all creditors.

schedule of accounts receivable. A list of each charge customer, the balance in the customer's account, and the total amount due from all customers.

small-volume builder. A home builder with 25 or fewer closings per year.

small-volume builder with land costs. A small-volume builder who only builds speculative or presold homes on lots the builder owns.

small-volume builder without land costs. A home builder with 25 or fewer closings per year who builds only on land the customer owns.

small-volume combination builder. A home builder with 25 or fewer closings per year who builds both speculative/presold homes on his or her own land and custom homes on customers' land.

working capital. Current assets of a business that can be applied to its current operations; current assets minus current liabilities.